POLITICAL
SOCIALIZATION

D1611922

The Little, Brown Series
in Comparative Politics

Under the Editorship of
GABRIEL A. ALMOND
JAMES S. COLEMAN
LUCIAN W. PYE

AN ANALYTIC STUDY

POLITICAL SOCIALIZATION

Second Edition

Richard E. Dawson
Washington University

Kenneth Prewitt
University of Chicago

Karen S. Dawson
Washington University

Boston   Toronto
LITTLE, BROWN AND COMPANY

Copyright © 1977, 1969 by Little, Brown and Company (Inc.)

All rights reserved. No part of this book may be reproduced in any form or by any electronic or mechanical means including information storage and retrieval systems without permission in writing from the publisher, except by a reviewer who may quote brief passages in a review.

Library of Congress Catalog Card No. 76-29538

ISBN 0-316-17741-5

6   5   4   3

HAL

Published simultaneously in Canada
by Little, Brown & Company (Canada) Limited

Printed in the United States of America

For Drew, Katie, Eric, Jennifer, and Geoffrey

Foreword

The second edition of *Political Socialization* is substantially a new book. What was a relatively new empirical discipline in the 1960s has become a major field of political science research and teaching in the 1970s, and this edition will serve as a comprehensive and insightful introduction into the field.

Political socialization research has not only been enriched by empirical and systematic studies in recent years; it has also become one of the most controversial subjects. In this text, the debates about the direction of causality as between political institutions and political culture, and about the relative importance of childhood socialization and adult experience are objectively presented and tested against the research evidence.

As in the first edition, the authors draw richly from the literature of political theory, comparative politics, and the other social sciences, and convey these theories and findings in simple, straightforward prose that will make *Political Socialization* an ideal teaching tool.

Gabriel A. Almond
James D. Coleman
Lucian W. Pye

Preface

Although in some respects traceable to the Greeks, the study of political socialization is more clearly rooted in the social revolutions of the eighteenth century. It was then that the citizen-at-large became more than a shadow figure on the political stage. Not until then did social observers give much attention to what the man on the street thought or how he came to hold those thoughts. With industrialization of the economic order and democratization of the political order, however, social theorists quickly recognized that the views of the masses could make a difference. The social order depends as much on the moods and the manners of the public as on inscribed laws or elite behavior. Indeed, as described by Rousseau, the social order rests upon a law that is

> graven neither on marble nor on brass, but in the hearts of the citizens; a law which creates the real constitution of the state, which acquires new strength daily, which, when other laws grow obsolete or pass away, revives them or supplies their place, preserves a people in the spirit of their institutions, and imperceptibly substitutes the force of habit for that of authority. I speak of manner, customs, and above all of opinion.

It is a natural step from Rousseau's observation to a corollary issue: How does the citizen come to believe what he does about the public order? Through what processes and with what consequences are political habits "graven in the hearts of the citizens"? These are the central questions of political socialization theory. A person "matures" politically just as he matures biologically or socially. Political learning begins early in life, much earlier than most theorists may believe. The "apprentice citizen" is being shaped by political socialization long before he reaches chronological adulthood and is given full legal status as a citizen.

Although this fact has been generally accepted for some time, systematic investigation is recent. The earliest major attempts to investigate the political learning process were published in 1931, in the influential series edited by Charles E. Merriam, *The Making of Citizens: A Comparative Study of Methods of Civic Training*. But sustained efforts to understand "the making of citizens" were not launched until the mid-1950s. Political researchers, stimulated by the behavioral revolution and outfitted with the tools of survey analysis, only then began to relate systematically political socialization processes to theories about political life. Within the last decade, scholars have collected the information, formed the hypotheses, and suggested the theories linking political learning to explanations of the public order.

In this text we attempt to draw together the ideas and data about political socialization. The book is designed to introduce the student of politics to the field of political socialization and to emphasize the close relationship between processes that "engrave laws in the hearts of citizens" and the larger social order. Although our discussion mainly depends on data gathered by others, we avoid any attempt at a systematic review or a propositional inventory of research findings. This book should be read as a map not designed to answer all questions about the terrain, but to organize and integrate enough features of the landscape to guide the new traveler as he begins his exploration.

This seems like an appropriate time to prepare a new edition of *Political Socialization*. In the first edition, arguments were based on a few pioneering studies. Since that time, the culmination of political events and many new research efforts have raised questions about ideas presented in the first edition.

Although the basic structure of the second edition of *Political Socialization* is the same as the earlier edition, much of the content is changed. It represents a major rewriting of the first edition, and incorporates and responds to the additional thinking and work in the field. Much new data about political socialization processes have been compiled in recent years; but we would caution the reader that many of the important questions and issues raised in this field are still open to investigation.

We wish to express appreciation to Alan Stern for reviewing and commenting on the first draft of the manuscript, and to Mary A. De Vries for a careful and efficient job of editing.

Richard E. Dawson
Kenneth Prewitt
Karen S. Dawson

Contents

CHAPTER I

Political Socialization and Political Life

POLITICAL SOCIALIZATION is concerned with the personal and social origins of political outlooks. The political life of any nation has both differences and similarities in political attachments, feelings about politics, and evaluations of leaders and policies. Citizens within a given nation share a common sense of national identity and loyalty that distinguishes them from citizens of other nations. But they may have diverse feelings about the effectiveness of their political leaders. Political socialization helps account for both the commonalities and diversities of political life.

Most people identify themselves as part of a particular nation. They develop a sense of loyalty to that nation. Such identities are among the most potent social ties. In both ancient and contemporary literature disloyalty to one's tribe, people, or nation has been portrayed as among the heinous of deeds.

Some individuals participate actively in political life. They vote, attend political meetings, contact public officials, and express their political involvement in numerous ways. Others are little involved. Such variations reflect, in part, differences in political systems. Some regimes promote widespread participation. Others limit participation to only a few. Differences in participation are related also to personal experiences and needs. Some people trust and respect their political leaders and processes. Others look at politics with indifference, distrust, or a sense of alienation.

1

Some people develop commitments to different ideologies. They identify with different political parties or groups. "I am a socialist." "I belong to the Democratic party." "I am a conservative." "I am a Marxist." "I am in the women's rights movement." These expressions of self-identification are indicative of involvements in political groups. But many people remain uncommitted and uninvolved.

How and why do most individuals come to identify with the nation? Why do some develop a sense of involvement in politics, while others do not? How and when and why do people acquire commitments to particular groups or ideologies? These are important questions for understanding political life. They are particularly significant for one seeking to understand relationships between a political system and its individual constituents. These issues are the focus of political socialization.

Questions such as these have long been of interest to those concerned with politics. From the earliest days political leaders have asked how a sense of loyalty to the state can be developed and maintained among the citizenry. They have sought to establish the legitimacy of a given regime and to maintain trust in themselves as its leaders. Political leaders have manipulated symbols, offices, and policies to insure support for themselves and their successors.

Political theorists have paid attention to the same questions. They have asked how given regimes can maintain the status quo or institute change through the education and manipulation of the citizenry. Political theorists as diverse as Plato [1] and Machiavelli [2] have stressed the importance of appropriate sentiments among the citizenry as crucial ingredients for political unity and order, a goal each sought in the context of his own time. Both Plato and Machiavelli developed notions of how political leaders should act to promote support and loyalty. In suggesting how to create and maintain the "good society," Plato described a system of political education, censorship, and propaganda. This system was de-

---

[1] Plato, *The Republic*.

[2] Machiavelli, *The Prince* (New York: The New American Library, 1952).

signed to promote loyalty to the state and to give legitimacy to a regime Plato considered "just." In advising the Prince on how to acquire and maintain power, Machiavelli instructed the Prince on how to act to command the respect and loyalty — although not necessarily the love — of his subjects.[3]

Social institutions often have taken on roles in shaping the outlooks of the citizenry. They, too, have acted upon the assumption that what citizens know, value, and expect from political life has consequences for the quality and form of the state. Religious institutions have used their influence to shape the political values of believers. More often than not they have taught obedience and acceptance of the existing political order. Occasionally religious groups have advocated alternatives to the established regime.

Educational leaders generally have defined shaping the outlooks of future citizens as part of their task. They, too, have sought to influence the maturing citizen in the direction of loyalty toward the existing order. The following statement by a superintendent of schools shows the self-conscious acceptance of political education:

> The public school is the greatest and most effective of all Americanization agencies. This is the one place where all children in a community or district, regardless of nationality, religion, politics, or social status, meet and work together in a cooperative and harmonious spirit. . . . The children work and play together, they catch the school spirit, they live the democratic life, American heroes become their own, American history wins their loyalty, the Stars and Stripes, always before their eyes in the school room, receives their daily salute. Not only are these immigrant children Americanized through the public school, but they, in turn, Americanize their parents carrying into the home many lessons of democracy learned at school.[4]

These examples demonstrate that questions of how individuals come to have particular political outlooks are important. They have been discussed since the earliest days of

---

3 *Ibid.*
4 Quoted in Robert A. Dahl, *Who Governs?* (New Haven: Yale University Press, 1961), pp. 317–318.

political life. They have been deemed important by those directly involved in political life and those who have sought to understand it in a more abstract sense. In this sense political socialization is a very old area of inquiry.

RECENT ATTENTION TO POLITICAL SOCIALIZATION: TWO LINES OF INQUIRY

Over the past two decades students of politics have focused systematically upon the origins of political outlooks. Using the techniques of empirical science and concepts and theories borrowed from other social scientists, they have investigated *how* and *when* and *why* individuals come to have particular political outlooks. From a small beginning in the late 1950s research and analysis on the development of political orientations has grown into a major area in the discipline of political science.

This contemporary concern with political socialization was the outcome of several trends in political analysis in the period following World War II. Two distinct areas of concern motivated this contemporary focus. The term came into use simultaneously in two lines of inquiry, suggested in the above discussion. On the one hand, inquiry into political socialization has been motivated by a desire to understand the bases for various patterns of individual political outlooks. On the other hand, the concept has been employed to analyze processes and characteristics of political systems. These two areas of inquiry are interrelated. Historically they contributed independently to the study of political socialization. A brief description of the two foci makes clearer the meaning of the concept, its place in political life and inquiry, and different approaches and emphasis in the field.

FOCUS UPON INDIVIDUAL ORIENTATIONS

Over the past half century students of politics have probed systematically the patterns of individual political attitudes and behavior. Who votes and who does not vote? How and why do people get involved in politics? What types of people are likely to be liberals? Conservatives? Radicals? How much does the average citizen know about the operation of his or her government, and to what extent is he or she interested in political life? Interest in these issues has been stimulated in part by the spread of the democratic ideology, or what might be called the "participation explosion" in politics, which has occurred in the twentieth century. Research on these patterns also has been facilitated by the development of survey sampling, interviewing, questionnaire design, opinion and personality measurement, and data processing techniques over the past four decades. By the late 1950s social scientists had accumulated a great deal of information on how voting behavior and political attitudes are related to economic, social, and psychological conditions.[5] Patterns of political interest and participation also had been explored.[6]

As this knowledge grew students of politics became interested in probing deeper into how people developed national identities, came to possess particular ideological commitments, acquired varying amounts of political interest and knowledge, and developed preferences for particular policies or programs. It was not enough for one to know that adults tended to maintain a constant identification with one political party. One wanted to know how and when that party identification was acquired and what factors contributed to its stability. The role of the family, the schools, group experiences, and communication media in the formation of political outlooks have served as subjects of investigation. In this line of inquiry the central question has been how and when and why individuals come to possess their particular political outlooks.

The first important work in this area was Herbert H. Hyman's *Political Socialization*.[7] The book, published in 1959, presented an inventory of research findings bearing on the

---

[5] See, for example, Seymour M. Lipset, *Political Man* (Garden City, N.Y.: Doubleday, 1960); and Bernard R. Berelson, Paul F. Lazarsfeld, and William N. McPhee, *Voting* (Chicago: The University of Chicago Press, 1954).

[6] See, for example, Robert E. Lane, *Political Life: Why People Get Involved in Politics* (Glencoe, Ill.: The Free Press, 1959); and Lester Milbrath, *Political Participation: How and Why Do People Get Involved in Politics* (Chicago: Rand McNally, 1965).

[7] Herbert Hyman, *Political Socialization* (Glencoe, Ill.: The Free Press, 1959).

sources of political outlooks. The findings, from a wide range of empirical studies, were organized and analyzed to pose and answer questions pertaining to the learning of political outlooks. Hyman began his discussion with the proposition that political behavior can be investigated fruitfully as one form of learned behavior. He noted how the more specific concern with political socialization stemmed from the attempt to identify patterns of political behavior:

> Regularities in the political behavior of adult individuals and stable differences between groups of adults have become a commonplace in social research. Such patterns of behavior may well be interpreted in terms of contemporaneous features present in the adult lives of particular individuals or groups. But, certainly it is true that the *continuity* of such patterns over time and place suggests that the individual has been modified in the course of his development in such a way that he is likely to exhibit certain persistent behavior apart from transient stimulation in his contemporary environment. One is naturally directed to the area of *learning;* more specifically to the *socialization* of the individual, his learning of social patterns corresponding to his societal positions as mediated through various agencies of society. One searches therefore for psychological studies which will establish the beginning of political behavior in pre-adult life, the process by which it emerges, and the subsequent changes in the course of further experiences.[8]

This early statement contains several notions important to political socialization inquiry. Note, in particular, the emphasis upon preadult experiences as antecedents for adult political behavior. The idea that political learning has its origins in early life and that what happens during childhood is important for shaping the political outlooks of later life have been major premises in the analysis of political socialization.

In 1960, a year after the publication of Hyman's book, reports from two field studies of the development of political orientations among American children were published.[9] Both

[8] *Ibid.,* pp. 25–26.

[9] See Fred I. Greenstein, "The Benevolent Leader: Children's Image of Political Authority," *American Political Science Review,* LIV (1960), pp. 934–945; and Robert D. Hess and David Easton, "The Child's Changing Image of the President," *Public Opinion Quarterly,* XXIV (1960), pp. 632–644.

studies traced the development of political outlooks of samples of American school children over the grammar school years. They focused on orientations toward political authority and emphasized the role of the presidency as a central focus in the political maturation of young Americans. These two studies have served as a foundation for much of the subsequent research and discussion on political learning among the young.[10]

POLITICAL SOCIALIZATION AS A TASK OF THE POLITICAL SYSTEM

As the concept of political socialization was being adopted by students probing patterns of individual political orientations, it also came into use in a line of inquiry that sought to understand properties and processes of political systems. Like other developments in the academic study of politics, this line of inquiry was influenced by events in the actual political world. Following World War II the world witnessed significant increases in the amount and rapidity of social and political change. Old empires and coalitions were disintegrated. The number of independent states grew rapidly in the wake of the breakup of European colonial empires. Other nations were altered radically by various forms of economic, social, and political change. Industrialization, economic development, modernization, and political development became major concerns to statesmen and scholars. Students of politics began to pay more attention to patterns of change and stability, to processes of political integration and disintegration. They also began to take heed of politics in the non-Western areas. They found that concepts and theories developed to analyze pre-World War II Western nations were not always adequate to analyze mid-twentieth-century political developments, much of it occurring outside the West. These new developments called for the asking of new questions. New questions required new concepts.

[10] See Fred I. Greenstein, *Children and Politics* (New Haven: Yale University Press, 1965); Robert D. Hess and Judith V. Torney, *The Development of Political Attitudes in Children* (Chicago: Aldine, 1967); and David Easton and Jack Dennis, *Children in the Political System: Origins of Political Legitimacy* (New York: McGraw-Hill, 1969).

A line of inquiry that followed from these concerns was the analysis of the conditions and processes that gave stability to some political systems and rendered others unstable. Inquiry into political socialization was developed as one way of exploring such issues. Political socialization was viewed from the standpoint of the political system instead of the individual. The main objective was to account for differences in the performance of political systems rather than differences or similarities in individual political outlooks. Political socialization was viewed as a process of the political system, one that had consequences for the functioning of the system. In the late 1950s two frameworks for analyzing political systems were proposed. One was the general system approach developed largely by David Easton.[11] The other was a framework of structural functional analysis introduced to the study of politics by Gabriel Almond and his associates.[12]

In both approaches political socialization is viewed as a means for developing support for the political system. It is a process through which appropriate values and knowledge regarding a particular political system are created among its constituents. Basic support is presumed necessary for a political system to persist over time. Easton and Robert Hess interpret the importance of political socialization as follows:

> But regardless of the specific devices any system utilizes to perpetuate itself no system is able to function, much less maintain itself for any length of time, without educating its young politically in the broadest sense of the meaning of these terms. Either intuitively or consciously it must undertake to transmit some of its political heritage to the maturing members of the society or to construct a new heritage for them so that a system that is undergoing serious transformations may anticipate future supports.[13]

[11] For early formulations of this, see David Easton, "An Approach to the Analysis of Political Systems," *World Politics*, LXV (1956–57), pp. 383–400; and David Easton, "Youth in the Political System," in Seymour Lipset and Leo Lowenthal (eds.), *Culture and Social Character* (New York: The Free Press, 1961), pp. 226–251.

[12] See, in particular, Gabriel Almond and James S. Coleman (eds.), *The Politics of the Developing Areas* (Princeton: Princeton University Press, 1960).

[13] Easton and Hess, *op. cit.*, p. 230.

Note again the emphasis upon shaping the political outlooks of the young. The system approach also postulates the
universality of system functions such as political socialization.
Both the Easton scheme and the Almond approach identify
functions they presume are performed by all political systems
regardless of specific political forms, historical or geographical
location, or stage of development.

In approaching political socialization from a structural
functional perspective, Almond specifies political socialization as one of seven functions performed by political systems.[14] The political analyst seeks to ascertain what
structures carry out the political socialization function. In
some instances the family may be the most important structure. In others the educational system may play the most
important role. Almond defines political socialization and
identifies the content of what is accomplished through political socialization as follows:

> What do we mean by the function of political socialization?
> We mean that all political systems tend to perpetuate their
> cultures and structures through time, and that they do this
> mainly by means of socializing influences of the primary and
> secondary structures through which the young of the society
> pass in the process of maturation. . . .
>   Political socialization is the process of induction into the
> political culture. Its end product is a set of attitudes, cogni-
> tions, value standards, and feelings — toward the political
> system, its various roles, and role incumbents. It also includes
> knowledge of, values affecting, and feelings toward the inputs
> of demands and claims into the system and its authoritative
> outputs.[15]

This is not the place for a critique of these two approaches.
In Chapter II we attempt to show how political socialization
has been used to deal with important system level questions.
Several common threads and important aspects can be cited
to clarify further the system usage of political socialization.
In both schemes the major theoretical concern is with the po-

---

[14] Gabriel Almond, "A Functional Approach to Comparative Politics,"
in Almond and Coleman, *op. cit.,* pp. 26–58.
[15] *Ibid.,* pp. 27–28.

litical system, not with individual attitudes and behavior per se. Both approaches assume that the types of political information, values, attitudes, and expectations citizens have about their politics have an impact upon how the political system operates. Both Almond and Easton conceptualize the political system as working to build and maintain support among its constituents. The system does this through educating the citizenry to accept the existing political order, to trust a given leadership, and to expect particular types of policies. They both see the passing on of appropriate political orientations to the young, maturing citizens as a particularly important part of this process.

Contemporary concern with political socialization has grown out of inquiry into these two distinct areas of political analysis: concern for the individual and concern for the system. Despite distinctions in basic focus there is much in common in these conceptualizations of political socialization. Both inquire into the development of political outlooks among individuals. Both place emphasis upon learning in the pre-adult years. The two perspectives are complementary. An important potential of the concept in the study of political life is that it ties analysis of the individual with the analysis of how political systems operate. The operation of the political system is seen as dependent on the political outlooks of the citizenry. The distributions of political outlooks among the citizenry are shaped, in part, by the needs, structures, and processes of the political system. In Chapter II we suggest ways in which political socialization can be tied into more explicit theories of political system behavior.

One additional aspect of political socialization should be reiterated. Political socialization is an approach to understanding *both* patterns of similarities and differences in political outlooks among the constituents of a given system. On the one hand, political socialization helps one to understand the development and dissemination of consensus values or common outlooks. For example, how is it that most residents of the United States come to identify themselves as Americans? Frenchmen develop high levels of loyalty toward France. The vast majority of Americans believe in democracy, at least as an abstract idea.[16] These common identities serve to tie the members of a nation together and to differentiate them from other nations.

On the other hand, political socialization is also an approach to understanding the differences in political perspectives that exist among constituents of the same state. With respect to many political issues, there can be great divisions among citizens who share a common national identity. Most Frenchmen identify themselves as French, but they may have very different interpretations of what it means to be French. Levels of political involvement vary greatly among the citizenry of an existing state. Members of different subgroups within a common national culture often have different expectations as to what political leaders should or should not do. Political socialization is a tool for understanding these intranation differences as well as for intranation similarities and internation differences.

The past decade and a half have seen a massive growth in studies and discussions of political socialization.[17] The use of the concept has made its way from the research designs and conceptual schemes of scholars at the frontier of the discipline to the curricula of advanced courses in political analysis, to basic undergraduate courses and textbooks. As is common in intellectual inquiry, the initial amassing of much additional information on a particular subject of inquiry can have mixed consequences. It can be said that the extensive research of the past decade has provided the student of politics with much more information about the processes of political socialization. But it has also left him with less understanding of the process than he had after the initial research. With relatively little information one could make assertions of basic patterns of processes with considerable assurance. Some of the bold assertions made following the early research have been qualified, refined, rejected, or seriously questioned by the results of

16 See James W. Prothro and Charles M. Grigg, "Fundamental Principles of Democracy: Bases of Agreement and Disagreement," *Journal of Politics,* 22 (May 1960), pp. 276–294.

17 For a recent bibliography of political socialization research, see Jack Dennis, *Political Socialization Research: A Bibliography* (Beverly Hills: Sage Publications, 1973).

additional studies. The patterns of political learning appear to be more complex and variable than was assumed earlier.[18] Basic "givens" of the early thinking, such as the dominant role of the family, the simple transmission of political outlooks from the older generation to the younger, and the centrality of early learning for shaping adult political outlooks, have been called to question. After more than a decade and a half of extensive discussion and investigation, few of the major questions pertaining to political socialization have been determined or put to rest.

OUTLINE AND DEVELOPMENT OF BOOK

In the following chapters we attempt to describe the process of political socialization. Our discussion rests upon the research and thinking done by others. We develop our argument around three basic questions: (1) What is the outcome of political socialization for the individual? For the political system? (2) When and how does political learning take place? (3) Who does the teaching? What parts do various social groups and associations, such as the family, the schools, the communication media, play in political socialization?

In the next two chapters we look at the outcomes of political socialization. In Chapter II we explore ideas regarding the implications of political socialization for the political system. How can processes of political learning by individuals be systematically related to properties and activities of political systems? In Chapter III we focus on the implications of political socialization for the individual. What does political learning mean for the individual? What are the components and the structure of one's political outlooks? We suggest the notion of the political self as a means of focusing on important substantive and developmental aspects of political learning.

In the next three chapters we look at developmental and

[18] For works that call into question some of the assumptions made in these early works, see R. W. Connell, "Political Socialization and the American Family: The Evidence Re-examined," *Public Opinion Quarterly*, 36 (Fall 1972), pp. 323–333; and Donald D. Searing, Joel J. Schwartz, and Alden E. Lind, "The Structuring Principle: Political Socialization and Belief Systems," *American Political Science Review*, 67 (June 1973), pp. 415–432.

learning processes. In Chapter IV we discuss early political learning. When does political learning begin? When and in what types of sequences does the individual pick up his or her outlooks about politics? Is there a particular developmental process to political learning? In Chapter V we look at political socialization during the adult years. How significant is the earlier learning in determining adult political outlooks? How much additional political learning or change occurs during the later years? Chapter VI investigates the techniques through which individuals take on political information, values, and attitudes. Distinctions are made between direct and indirect political learning. Different types of processes are identified.

In the next section we deal with the various societal agents or associations that play roles in political socialization. Through what types of group experiences does one learn about the political world and develop his or her particular attachments to and evaluations of it. In Chapter VII we look at the role of the family. Chapter VIII explores the impact of schools and educational experiences. In Chapter IX the role of social groups is investigated. Distinctions are made between primary groups, secondary groups, and societal groupings, and the varying ways in which they affect political learning. Chapter X discusses the impact of the communication media and of experiences the individual has with the political world. Political events can shape or alter political attachments and evaluations. The types of experiences an individual has as he or she participates in political activities may shape his or her feelings concerning the fairness and responsiveness of political processes, as well as his or her own feeling of efficacy regarding politics.

CHAPTER II

Political Socialization and the Political System

THE POLITICAL SYSTEM AND POLITICAL SOCIALIZATION

In the last chapter we suggested that political socialization has consequences for both the individual and the political system. In this chapter we look at political socialization from the perspective of the political system as a whole. Here we ask about the larger political consequences that result from the way that a whole nation of citizens acquires its political views. From this perspective the following types of questions can be raised: Is a nation governed by democratic rules? Is a nation marked by cooperative relations among its different races and ethnic groups? Is a nation troubled by outbreaks of political violence? The assumption is made that the governing rules, the level of harmony and cooperation, and the stability of political life are somehow rooted in the political socialization of a population.

To help clarify the distinction between the individual and the system level of analysis we present Table II. 1. It shows the different ways a political concept might be used depending on the level of analysis. From the system perspective political socialization can be defined as the process through which citizens acquire political views *that become aggregated* in ways that have consequences for the political life of the nation.

TABLE II.1   *Use of Political Concept According to Individual and System Level of Analysis*

Political Concept	Individual-Level Analysis of Political Socialization	System-Level Analysis of Political Socialization
Loyalty	Does a child learn to trust and have confidence?	In trying to get citizens to obey the law does the government depend on the loyalty and patriotism of citizens, or must it use force and coercion?
Tolerance	As citizens grow up do they accept or reject members of different races, ethnic background, regions, religions, and so on?	Are national politics characterized by cooperation or conflict among the social groups that make up the society?
Democracy	What meaning does a citizen attach to the act of voting?	Is there widespread intelligent political participation in choosing the authorities and shaping the policies that govern the nation?

The italicized phrase needs further clarification. What is meant by "becomes aggregated?" Consider the analogy of voting and elections. *Voting* is something individual citizens do. We can study voting by investigating what kinds of citizens vote Republican and what kinds vote Democratic; we can examine the motives citizens bring to the polling booth; we can even study voting by finding out who does not vote. But studying whether people vote, how they vote, and why they vote that way tells us very little about elections.

The study of *elections* is the study of which political party wins — how frequently and by what margin. It is the study of whether the party that wins control of the White House is also the party that wins control of Congress. It is the study of how new public policies or changes in the elite or modifications of the basic constitutional rules might vary depending on electoral outcomes. These broad political questions cannot be answered by looking at individual voters. They can be answered only when the voting behavior (including nonvoting) of millions of citizens is aggregated into an electoral outcome. It is the outcome or result of elections that has consequences for the entire political system.

The convenient thing about voting and elections is that there is an automatic and quickly understood "aggregating mechanism." A vote becomes politically meaningful when it is counted and added to other votes. This counting and adding is the aggregation. Because the election result aggregates millions of individual votes the political scientist moves easily from the level of individual analysis (the vote) to the level of the nation-state analysis (election outcomes).

If this example makes clear what is meant by aggregating individual behavior it also emphasizes the difficulty facing the student of political socialization. There is no automatic or obvious aggregating mechanism. There is no simple way to add together millions of individual political socialization experiences and come up with a "political socialization outcome" that has identifiable and meaningful consequences for the entire political system. What does it mean for the political life of the nation to learn that 78 percent of a sample of first-graders and 42 percent of a sample of fifth-graders think that the president is the most important political figure in the nation? What broad political consequences follow from a finding that high school civics and history courses do not influence student political views? Do we learn anything about the larger issues of political stability or democratic government when we learn that most American children acquire a political party identification from their parents rather than from their teachers or friends?

The task of political socialization theory is to take such specific findings and link them to an interpretation of the broad political issues of stability, democracy, party competition, justice, equality. At least this is the task if political socialization findings are to take on meaning beyond the level of explaining individual political views or behaviors.

In the remainder of this chapter we review different political theories of political socialization. *A political theory of political socialization* attempts to state the relevance of socialization for the way in which the political system operates.

Applying the language used earlier, we can define it as a theory that aggregates or combines individual political socialization experiences so explanations about the nation-state as a whole can be advanced.

Although the theories we review are not without flaws and ambiguities, our review is not critical. It is enough of a job just to understand how the theories are put together, and how they make use of socialization findings. The theories are introduced here primarily to illustrate that political socialization has meaning beyond the level of the individual citizen. Our review focuses on two broad theories: the "systems theory" and the "hegemonic theory" of political socialization.

SYSTEMS THEORY OF POLITICAL SOCIALIZATION

Systems theory in political science has been elaborated in the writing of David Easton.[1] Easton and his colleague Jack Dennis have applied systems theory to the study of political socialization.[2] Systems theory in general and its application in particular constitute a broad, complex topic. In these few pages we consider only those parts of the topic that help us answer our immediate question: in what respects does political socialization have consequences for the political life of the entire nation?

WHAT IS SYSTEMS THEORY?

According to Easton, the very persistence of political systems is problematic. There is no law given by nature or by a metaphysical being that requires a collection of people to organize themselves politically in a particular manner and then to remain faithful to that organization. People may one day decide that democratic elections are the best method of choosing leaders, and the next day decide that leaders should be chosen by lot. Or there may be sentiment at one time that all persons

[1] For a full discussion of systems analysis of politics, see David Easton, *A Framework for Political Analysis* (Englewood Cliffs, N.J.: Prentice-Hall, 1965); and *A Systems Analysis of Political Life* (New York: Wiley, 1965).

[2] David Easton and Jack Dennis, *Children in the Political System: Origins of Political Legitimacy* (New York: McGraw-Hill, 1969).

living in what is now the continental United States belong to the same nation; later the prevailing sentiment might be that persons living east of the Mississippi River should belong to a different nation than persons living west of it. The American Civil War was an unsuccessful attempt to split one nation into two nations, just as the founding period was a successful attempt to transform thirteen "nations" into one nation.

In his systems theory Easton directs attention to a critical fact. Political systems do tend to persist through time. That is, the group of people who at one time consider themselves as belonging to the same national political community tend to continue to believe that, as do their children after them. Similarly, the basic set of constitutional rules that govern the nation at one time tend to govern it at subsequent times. Clearly these rules are modified — in United States political history there have been constitutional amendments that have modified the responsibilities of key institutions, the definition of citizenship, and how government leaders are selected. But these modifications have left intact the basic constitutional principles such as federalism, separation of powers, majoritarianism, civilian control of the military, first amendment freedoms, and the like. Persistence and change are not incompatible in systems theory, as long as the change leaves intact the basic manner in which valued things are allocated to the population.

Although persistence is the normal condition of political systems, it cannot be taken for granted. For one thing, political systems are often placed under stress by virtue of what they do — reward and punish. People who get punished rather than rewarded are not likely to be happy about it. People who pay high taxes and get few benefits, for example, are being deprived by the government. When the laws of a society allow some groups to get the best jobs, the highest incomes, and the most influential positions, while others do menial labor at low wages and never become influential, the political system has rewarded some groups and punished others. Slave systems are exaggerated illustrations of this, but less exaggerated cases such as sexism or racism or ethnic discrimination are no less real to the penalized groups.

Easton is interested in how political systems manage to persist despite their engaging in activities that differentially reward and punish groups in society. One explanation, he argues, is that people grant support to the political system. Support is the trust, confidence, and affection persons attach to other persons or objects. Withdrawal of support is expressed as mistrust, lack of confidence, or hostility. We support the college authorities when we have confidence that they are trying to act in our behalf or when we like and respect them. We do not support them when we think they cannot be trusted or are incompetent or fail to merit our respect.

In systems theory there are different kinds of support that become important. There is specific support. Persons grant *specific support* when they are getting something concrete in return. A worker says: "I am loyal to and vote for the Democrats because wages go up when they run the government." This worker is granting specific support (loyalty and his vote) to a political object (Democratic party) on a *quid pro quo* basis — you scratch my back, I'll scratch yours.

There is also *diffuse support,* which is unconditional support. It is the generalized trust and confidence citizens grant to political authorities or objects — a "my country, right or wrong" kind of feeling. Patriotism and national loyalty are expressions of diffuse support. In times of war or economic hardship, for instance, citizens continue to feel loyal to their government even though specific benefits might be at low ebb. To say "I am a loyal American" often means a willingness to obey laws or make personal sacrifices even though no personal benefit is anticipated.

In systems theory, as outlined by Easton, diffuse support is the important social cement that keeps a political system together despite hard times and internal conflicts. To paraphrase Easton, diffuse support helps us understand why a political system is not always torn apart by the conflicts that occur as different groups try to increase their slice of the pie while shifting to other groups the hard work of baking the pie. It is through politics that different sized slices of pie are handed out; and it is at the urging of government that the effort it takes to create the pie is induced. No wonder, then, that something like diffuse support is necessary if political systems are to persist.

Easton and Dennis take the next step. They ask, where does diffuse support come from? Why is it that citizens form the kind of bond with political objects that leads to system persistence rather than system decay or disruption? Conversely, why is it that sometimes diffuse support is withdrawn? Why is it that some political systems do decay or experience severe disruption, even revolution?

For Easton and Dennis the answers to these questions are found in part in the study of political socialization. In the remainder of this section we summarize the arguments and evidence they present in *Children in the Political System*. Before undertaking this we emphasize our purpose. The study of political socialization wears two hats. First, how do people acquire the traits and viewpoints that make them this rather than that kind of political person — a voter rather than a nonvoter, a Democrat rather than a Republican, a patriot rather than a revolutionary, a conservative rather than a liberal? Second, what are the consequences of political socialization processes for the political system that result in a stable or volatile politics, a democratic or authoritarian regime, a just or an unjust rule? The systems theory of political socialization is very much about the consequences of political socialization for the political system, not the consequences for the individual citizen.

Easton and Dennis begin with a basic assumption about the consequences of early childhood political socialization: "Those children who begin to develop positive feelings toward the political authorities will tend to grow into adults who will be less easily disenchanted with the system than those children who early acquire negative, hostile sentiments."[3] Note that this is a probability statement. It is not claimed that all children who acquire positive feelings about political authorities will offer unswerving political support as adults. It is not claimed that every child who begins life with negative feelings matures into a political revolutionary. On balance, however, a society in which children acquire positive feelings will have

3 *Ibid.*, pp. 106–107.

a greater reservoir of diffuse support toward the political system than will a society in which children grow up distrusting and disliking political authorities.

The Easton and Dennis study analyzes what American grade school children learn and feel about political authorities. Their findings can be summarized under four headings: politicization, personalization, idealization and institutionalization.

Politicization. The infant has no image of politics; he or she makes no distinction between the private and public spheres. For the preschooler authority is almost exclusively the authority of the parent. Gradually, however, distinctions become possible. Early socialization processes "begin to pry the child away from exclusive bonds to the family and make it possible for him to reach out to the structure of political authority. He is able . . . to recognize the superior authority of the policeman, and to accept the higher power and performance qualities of political institutions when compared with the father." Easton and Dennis conclude that by grade 8 the typical American child is thoroughly politicized; "he has become aware of the presence of an authority outside of and more powerful than the family."[4] How is this political awareness acquired?

Personalization. Political awareness is acquired because particular political authorities are highly visible and salient to American children, notably two authorities: the president and the policeman. Government is not an abstraction to children. It is concrete, knowable persons. As Easton and Dennis put it, the child's "first glimpse of government is in the form of the President."[5] Personalization then, is the initial link between the child and the remote but significant world of political authority. What is the content of this link?

Idealization. The president, in particular, although also the policeman, is viewed by the young child as an idealized per-

[4] *Ibid.*, pp. 391–392.
[5] *Ibid.*, p. 139.

son. This is the basic Easton and Dennis finding. As viewed by children, the president is protective, helpful, trustworthy, intelligent, hardworking, persistent, correct in his judgments, and well qualified as a leader. In short, the president is idealized. The child commits himself or herself to the president; it is a commitment free of mistrust or criticism or indifference. Although this highly positive evaluation begins to erode as the child grows older, the initial attachment is overwhelmingly positive.

A summary of the Easton and Dennis argument indicates how their findings fit into a broader political theory. The first thing they report is that children begin at an early age to distinguish between private, family-rooted authority and public, government-rooted authority. However, it is surprising that there is not a similar distinction between the personal and impersonal. The public authority is practically as personal, intimate, and accessible as the private authority known in the family. This was the second finding, that public authority is initially intuited by the child in very personal terms. Third, the personalization of government is viewed through rose-tinted glasses. Government comes into the life of the child as a helpful and friendly person: the president and the local policeman. Easton and Dennis believe these findings "contain a hint about the source of diffuse support for the structure of authority, not among children alone but among adults as well. It is conceivable that idealization during the early years of life will leave a residue of positive sentiment within the later adult." [6] It is to this possibility that they next direct our attention.

Institutionalization. By what process would this idealization of political authorities be transformed into diffuse support for the political system? Concretely, a six-year-old child thinks that the president is a good guy. A forty-six-year-old citizen continues to pay taxes and support the government even when he disagrees with the policies it pursues. How do Easton and Dennis get from the six-year-old to the forty-six-year-old, from the naive trust to the mature patriotism? The

[6] *Ibid.,* p. 204.

key term in their theory is institutionalization. As the child grows up he or she begins to transfer positive feelings about the president to the institutions of government: to Congress, the Supreme Court, the executive branch, and so forth.

These institutions have a head start on claims to citizen affection and trust. The head start derives from the positive bond young children have already formed with political authority. Eventually, of course, these institutions will be judged in terms of how well they perform; and indeed, so will the president himself. If they perform effectively, the average citizen will show positive feelings. If they perform poorly, the average citizen will express negative feelings. *But,* the negative feelings are cushioned because the initial bond between citizen and authoritative institutions is strongly positive.

Now we come to the root of diffuse support. Diffuse support by adult citizens — feelings of political loyalty, patriotism, commitment, "my country, right or wrong" — emerge from the positive feelings shown toward the president and other political persons during the childhood years of growing political awareness. Moreover, this diffuse support enables a political system to persist despite severe strains imposed by the substantive policies of government. The strains result from the way that government both rewards and punishes, protects and coerces, and provides services and collects taxes. Even citizens who benefit less from, and those who pay more to, government than others continue to give diffuse support.

SUMMARY

We have attempted to outline in brief form a complicated and elaborate political theory of political socialization. Our goal has not been to accept it or to criticize it. There is much in the theory that is important and useful to the study of politics, just as there is much that is open to question and criticism. Some of the criticism will emerge as we pursue other topics.

Here the task has been to illustrate how political socialization can be more than an explanation of what and how children learn about politics. This is the impressive accomplishment of Easton and Dennis. They have applied political

socialization in a theory that sets out to explain one of the
most difficult of all political questions: how do governments
manage to persist even when, objectively, it appears that very
many of the citizens who pay taxes and obey laws might have
good reason to resist orders from a distant and often disliked
government? With this as the background question, Easton
and Dennis propose that the particular form in which American children initially learn about politics is related to the
more general problem of maintaining diffuse support for a
structure of political authority. Stated even more broadly,
their study advances a political theory of political socialization, a theory that connects the political socialization of children to the operation of political systems.

Although systems theory is sufficiently general that it can
encompass many other broad theories, it is instructive to give
particular attention to a theory that gives to political socialization certain emphases not found in the Easton and Dennis
study.

THE "HEGEMONIC THEORY" OF POLITICAL SOCIALIZATION

The word *hegemony* refers to domination or control. It is a
term used in political writing to describe the domination that
selected interests in society exercise over the whole of society.
Applied to political socialization the ideas of hegemony refer
to the way that groups with political power manipulate symbols and use propaganda and censorship to consolidate their
rule. A hegemonic theory of political socialization attempts to
demonstrate how political ideology is transmitted from the
dominant to the dominated groups in society.[7]

The idea of hegemony can be illustrated through an exam-

[7] The concept *hegemony* has been defined as "an order in which a
certain way of life and thought is dominant, in which one concept of
reality is diffused throughout society in all its institutional and private
manifestations, informing with its spirit all taste, morality, customs,
religious and political principles, and all social relations, particularly
in their intellectual and moral connotations." See Gwynn Williams,
"Gransci's Concept of *Egemonia*," *Journal of the History of Ideas*, 21,
no. 4 (1960), p. 587. An application of hegemonic theories can be found
in Ralph Miliband, *The State in Capitalist Society* (London: Edenfeld
and Nicolson, 1969), especially chs. 7 and 8. For a more explicit statement of how hegemonic ideas relate to political socialization, see Mario
B. Machado, "Political Socialization in Authoritarian Systems: The Case
of Brazil" (Ph.D. dissertation, University of Chicago, 1975). Many of the
ideas in the following paragraphs were stimulated by Machado's study.

ple. In capitalist countries the ownership of private property is a major source of political domination. Groups that own the industrial base of society (factories, transportation systems, communication networks, raw materials, etc.) are able to dominate nonowning groups. Moreover, it is in the interest of the dominant groups to get the nondominant groups to accept domination. In the capitalist example, it is in the interests of property owners to convince nonproperty owners that private ownership of basic production and services in society is both important and legitimate. If nonowners accept that private ownership is right and appropriate they are in effect accepting the rules and values by which they are dominated.

This example describes the most common theme in hegemonic theory, the theme of *class hegemony*. When the interests of one class (capitalists) are believed to represent the general interests of the nation, class hegemony is established. The marxist theorists who develop this argument believe the state plays an important role in safeguarding the domination of the capitalist class. The state does this in two respects: it uses force to insure that persons who question the economic arrangements do not receive much of a hearing. Political prisoners around the world can testify to the risks taken when the dominant class is questioned. The state also plays an important educating role. For example, by allowing citizens to participate in "harmless" ways, the state contributes to the allegiance citizens feel toward the very arrangements that dominate them.

Elitism is another variant of hegemonic theory. *Elite theory* stresses the dominant role of the ruling group. This group (and it may or may not represent the interests of a particular economic class) does all it can to insure its continued rule. Moreover, it attempts to pass on its privileges and powers to its offspring. Hereditary monarchies are the clearest example. But bureaucratic political parties (e.g., in the Soviet Union) or military dictatorships (e.g., in many Latin American countries) can also be the vehicle through which groups gain and then safeguard their dominance. As with class hegemony, elite hegemony uses the powers of the state, both coercive and educative, to preserve their control.

A hegemonic theory of political socialization, therefore,

emphasizes socialization processes and agencies that dominant groups use to get subservient groups to accept the social values and the social order that maintain the control relationships. It is clear that this theory shares certain assumptions with the systems theory earlier outlined. Both theories attempt to explain how particular patterns of authority persist through time. Both use notions from political socialization to build the explanation. It is possible to view hegemonic theory as a particular variant of system theory. But hegemonic theorists bring to political socialization an emphasis and a language that thus far have not emerged from the research literature guided by Easton's systems theory. It will help us understand hegemonic theory to view it as an alternative conception.

Hegemonic Theory as an Alternative Conception. If political socialization studies were to be guided by hegemonic concepts they would emphasize somewhat different processes and consequences than those found in the present literature.

Like systems theory, hegemonic theory starts with the assumption that government would not be possible unless the strains and tensions associated with the unequal allocation of values in society were somehow muted. Hegemonic theory, however, insists that the unequal allocation of values is persistently biased in favor of ruling classes or ruling groups. Systems theory allows for such a bias, but does not insist on it.

For a hegemonic theorist, then, there are always the same winners and always the same losers (at least in the pre-socialist state.) Unless the losers come to see that the way things are is "natural" or "appropriate" or "legitimate," social disruptions are likely. Socialization is viewed as the learning that leads the losers to accept the way things are, even to think that the way things are is in their best interests.

In the standard literature in political socialization, including the research reviewed in subsequent chapters of this text, the emphasis is on how political values are transmitted from one generation (the parent generation) to another (the new or younger generation). Socialization is the study of how parents influence children, how teachers instruct students, how

youth leaders provide behavioral models for youngsters, and
how materials written and prepared by adults are presented to
preadults. In the major agencies of political socialization,
families and schools, some members of the older generation
have substantial and direct responsibilities for what members
of the newer generation believe about themselves and their
society. In short, political socialization is the way in which
youth are brought into a political society established by preceding generations.

In hegemonic theory the political socialization process primarily identifies how political values are transmitted from the
dominant interests in society to the dominated groups. Socialization through time is less important than socialization
across power groups. Guided by hegemonic theory, the study
of political socialization asks how the ruled learn what the
rulers expect of them.

Discontinuities in Political Socialization. The term *discontinuities* refers to breaks in the flow of messages from the
agents of socialization to those being socialized. We need a
concept such as discontinuities to account for social change.
Without such a concept the social order would look now as it
always has looked. There would be perfect historical continuity. But of course there is not perfect historical continuity.
What people believe about politics in one historical period is
never completely reproduced in subsequent periods.

One form of discontinuity in political socialization occurs
when the younger generation either refuses to learn or is not
taught the basic political values of the older generation. The
key term is "generation gap," a term made famous in the
1960s. The *generation gap* occurs when the things believed
in and taught by the parental generation are rejected by the
children of that generation. For example, older generations in
America believed that patriotism required citizens to fight in
whatever wars or battles the political leadership declared to
be in the interests of the nation. In the 1960s many of the
younger generation rejected this belief. Thousands of college
youths actively protested the Vietnam War and hundreds of
youths deliberately avoided the military draft. This disconti-

nuity in values about patriotism and service to nation was widely reported as a generation gap.

In hegemonic theory there would be discontinuity in political socialization if ruled groups refused to learn or were not taught the basic political values fostered by the ruling group. Now the key term becomes *revolutionary challenge,* for when the ruled no longer accept as normal the arrangements by which they are ruled, the conditions necessary for revolution have been established. Again the America of the 1960s provides an illustration. Blacks have long been among the ruled groups in this society. From time to time there have been challenges to the racist arrangements that allowed whites always to rule over blacks, but until the 1960s these challenges were sporadic and generally put down by the police force at the disposal of the white ruling groups. In the 1960s the black power movement, urban guerrilla warfare, civil rights marches and demonstrations, and general political agitation by blacks became a much more serious challenge to racist political arrangements. Black groups along with sympathetic white groups prepared booklets and shouted slogans that announced a "counterideology" to the official ideology of the established ruling groups. We need not evaluate here the successes and failures of this challenge; we only point out that when a ruled group deliberately and consciously proposes a counterideology, this is evidence of discontinuity in political socialization.

Consequences of Political Socialization. In hegemonic theory effective political socialization leads to the stability of the ruling group. The arrangements that favor certain social and economic interests in society over other interests continue to favor those interests. A ruling group does not necessarily mean a particular set of people. Rulers can come and go, but the interests that dominate society continue to dominate it. For example, the capitalist class in the United States has ruled over wage earners and unskilled labor for more than a century. Certainly there has been much change during this century, including changes in the members of the ruling group. Nevertheless, so the argument goes, the basic relations between the dominant interests and the dominated group have been continuously reproduced.

Government in the Political Socialization Process. Hegemonic theory gives much emphasis to how the state self-consciously and deliberately mixes into the political socialization process. It does so primarily through propaganda and censorship.[8] Propaganda comes into play if the state is generally accepted. It is a technique that reaffirms the legitimacy of current authority relations. There are numerous methods of propaganda, including the widespread use of political ceremonies and symbols (flags, national heroes), the content of school textbooks, the attempt to associate government personnel and actions with majesty (the robes of judges and the hushed tones of the court), and the general speech making that celebrates the current political order.

Censorship comes into play when the legitimacy of the state is in doubt or is being actively challenged. The power of the state is used to manage the news, to quiet criticism, to deny a voice to groups challenging state authority, or to forbid public meetings or political demonstrations that aim "at the overthrow of the government." Censorship is not necessary if citizens either are politically indifferent or accept and support established ruling groups. Indeed, the relative mixture of propaganda and censorship is a useful index for determining whether there are serious challenges to the ruling interests. Over the past decade, for instance, the African nation of Kenya has steadily increased the amount of government censorship as more and more citizens have grown weary and then angry at the land and wealth amassed by the ruling groups.

The distinction between propaganda and censorship is less immediately important to us than how hegemonic theory differs in emphasis from the standard political socialization literature. Few socialization studies have given much attention to matters such as propaganda or censorship, presuming that the state is not an active intervenor in the socialization process. Political socialization occurs through millions and mil-

---

[8] This distinction between propaganda and censorship is applied in Machado, *op. cit.*

lions of interactions between the older generation and the younger generation. In contrast, hegemonic theory gives a good deal of attention to propaganda and censorship and to the active role played by the dominant interests in society. The millions of individual interactions between older and younger citizens is not as central to political socialization as is the deliberate manipulation of political symbols by the ruling class.

SUMMARY

A useful way to summarize hegemonic theory is to dwell on the phrase "my enemy is the government." It takes extraordinary political conditions before citizens could consciously accept the sentiment behind this phrase. The expected and by far most common citizen attitude is one that accepts the government as benign (helpful, useful, important, legitimate) or, at worst, as inevitable. The "enemy" in politics is the other political party, or the economic, racial, ethnic group that pushes unacceptable policies; or the regional group that is getting more than its share of the resources; or particular political authorities who use their positions to harm others and help themselves. Political parties, interest groups, social movements, and political authorities may from time to time and for certain excluded citizens be viewed as enemies. But this is far different from seeing the government itself as the enemy. The government is the basic structure of authority that allows a large number of people to live together as part of one collective unit. As long as people want to be part of that political community it is hard to see how these arrangements themselves can be the enemy.

Most people most of the time in most nations *do* support their respective governments. This is the historical fact with which any general theory of political socialization must deal. In dealing with this fact, theories that give emphasis to hegemony rather than to diffuse support operate under a particular burden.

In systems theory, with its emphasis on diffuse support, the reluctance of citizens to view the government as a political enemy is not problematic. After all, the government provides the structure within which a normal life is possible; a life in which citizens have jobs and earn a living, raise a family, enjoy hobbies, take trips, and see friends. However much a citizen might disagree with certain government policies of leaders, it would not be "rational" for him or her to actively challenge the government itself.

In hegemonic theory, with its emphasis on domination and control, the reluctance of citizens to view the government as a political enemy is "irrational" and thereby problematic. This reluctance has to be explained. After all, the government is in the service of a limited set of interests. These interests of the dominant groups are pursued at the expense of policies that would serve the interests of dominated groups. Because very many citizens belong to the dominated groups of society, it is difficult to see why they tolerate political arrangements that consistently penalize their interests. It is not rational for them to support a government under the control of interests opposed to their welfare.

Hegemonic theory, therefore, must come up with an explanation of behavior that can be taken for granted by systems theory. Hegemonic theory must explain why most of the time most of the people in most nations do accept political authority as legitimate, even though this acceptance is not in their own interests.

The explanation almost always introduces some variant of what, since Marx, has been called *false consciousness.* As applied in political socialization theories, this phrase describes the condition of large numbers of people accepting a social and political order even when it is not in their objective interests to do so. More specifically, false consciousness is used to explain why dominated groups accept as legitimate the very arrangements under which they are dominated. The reason that citizens seldom proclaim the state to be the enemy is that they have been lulled or fooled (socialized) into believing the state is not the enemy.

What hegemonic theorists must do, therefore, is explain how false consciousness comes about. This they do by invoking the ideas of propaganda (symbol manipulation) and censorship (selective control of information).

CONCLUSIONS

This chapter is a reminder that the study of political socialization involves more than explaining how individual citizens come to hold their particular political beliefs and goals. The student of politics also wants to understand how political socialization patterns contribute to the political life of the nation as a whole.

For the most part, in the chapters that follow the focus is upon the individual-level question. How do individuals acquire the political selves that guide and structure adult political beliefs and behavior? Most of the research and analysis of political socialization has been at the individual level. The reader should keep in mind, however, that the patterns and processes of individual political learning are of importance in political analysis because they have consequences for the collective political life.

CHAPTER III

The Political Self

MEANING OF POLITICAL SOCIALIZATION

What does it mean for an individual to be socialized into politics? What does an individual acquire from political socialization? How can one characterize the product of political socialization processes? Political socialization is one type of relationship the individual has with the political system in which he or she lives. One forms his or her particular political outlooks as a result of relationships he or she has with that political system and with various groups and individuals that are part of it.

At the individual level *political socialization* may be defined very simply as the processes through which an individual acquires his particular political orientations — his knowledge, feelings, and evaluations regarding his political world. We deliberately use the term "acquire" to stress that political socialization is an interactive process between the individual being socialized and the polity and societal agents that socialize him. Definitions that use terms such as "enculteration," "induction into," and "building in" suggest a passive role on the part of the individual. The role of society and the agents of socialization are overemphasized by such terms. "Learns," "takes on," and "adapts oneself" error in the opposite direction. They suggest a role too active or initiative for the individual becoming socialized. The role of the agents in constricting and molding the individual is underemphasized.

Political socialization can involve action on the part of both the individual and the socializing agents. Individuals both "socialize themselves" and "are socialized." Those who talk about political socialization often have very different notions of what happens in the process. Socialization is viewed by some as the transmission of political information, values, and perspectives from parents, teachers, and other socializing agents to new and maturing citizens. Others emphasize the developing capacity of the child to understand the political world. The former stresses what the agents of socialization pass on. The latter focuses upon the developing abilities of the individual. A comprehensive conception of political socialization must include both of these perspectives.

Different socialization experiences may stress one aspect over the other. In some instances individuals play a passive role. Outlooks are molded by the society and its agents. The young school child often is drilled in expressions of patriotism. The exercise of pledging allegiance to the flag at the beginning of the school day and assemblies that commemorate important events and birthdays are common parts of school curricula. They are deliberate efforts by the school to shape political attachments. In a similar manner young children are admonished by parents and teachers to respect and obey persons in positions of authority.

In these examples there is an attempt on the part of socialization agents such as the family and the school to shape the content of political outlooks. The norms of loyalty to nation and respect for authority are transmitted to potential citizens. The individuals being socialized have little choice in the content of the message or their exposure to it. Patriotic feelings and appreciation for the virtues of the nation are taught to the young so future adult citizens will be loyal to the nation. Young children are taught to respect authorities both so they can get along in a world characterized by authority relationships and so the society can anticipate compliance with its authoritative decisions.

In some instances the individual becoming socialized plays a more active or self-determining role. The fifteen-year-old perceives the political world differently from the seven-year-old, not so much because his exposure to the messages or agents of socialization is different, as because his innate capacity to comprehend political relationships is more developed. The adult citizen may come to distrust political authorities, not because his family or teachers taught him that they are not to be trusted, but because his own observations are that those in positions of authority have acted in bad faith or have fumbled in carrying out their responsibilities.

Political socialization is a special form of the more general phenomenon of socialization. The concept "socialization" was adopted into the study of politics from its use in other behavioral sciences — anthropology, psychology, social psychology, and sociology. Although the sources of the term lay in these other fields of study, the concept has not been applied to the study of politics without change. Students of politics have reformulated the concept so it fits better their own subject matter and theoretical interests. The reformulations are instructive in pointing out what occurs to the individual as he or she becomes socialized into politics.

Some of the early students of political socialization were influenced by the work of the cultural anthropologists and their conceptions of the socialization process.[1] The cultural anthropologists were among the first to study socialization as a key to understanding variations in personality, values, and social behavior among members of different societies. The work of the early cultural anthropologists was influenced by Freudian assumptions about personality development and the relationship between man and his society.[2] Childhood socialization—fre-

[1] For example, see Gabriel Almond, "A Functional Approach to Comparative Politics," in Gabriel Almond and James S. Coleman (eds.), *The Politics of the Developing Areas* (Princeton: University Press, 1960), pp. 3–64; Robert A. LeVine, "The Role of the Family in Authority Systems: A Cross-Cultural Application of Stimulus-Generalization Theory," *Behavioral Science*, V (1960), pp. 291–296; and Lucian W. Pye, *Politics, Personality, and Nation Building* (New Haven: Yale University Press, 1962).

[2] For example, see Allison Davis and John Dollard, *Children of Bondage* (Washington, D.C.: American Council on Education, 1940); Abram Kardiner and Ralph Linton, *The Individual and His Society* (New York: Columbia University Press, 1939); and J. W. M. Whiting and I. L. Child, *Child Training and Personality: A Cross-Cultural Study* (New Haven: Yale University Press, 1963).

quently referred to as child rearing or child training — was viewed from the Freudian perspective primarily as a mechanism through which the child's "antisocial" tendencies were brought under control. They argued that civilization is possible only if the child learns that he cannot replace his father, marry his sister, take his neighbor's belongings, or engage in other often tempting "antisocial" behavior. Society and its representatives, through their socialization mechanisms, suppress or redirect what are often regarded as the child's "natural" tendencies. The process of socialization further acts to help the individual rationalize and justify the sacrifices he or she must make to become a part of society. Socialization from this prospective ushers the individual into society as it forces him to shed his "antisocial" inclinations.

Students of culture and personality saw that socialization involved other things as well. They pointed out that the child is also developed as he is socialized. He learns the technology of his society. He is introduced to its cultural lore and traditions. He is instructed in his rights and duties. He becomes a part of social relationships. As George Herbert Mead pointed out, a self is formed as the basic product of socialization of the individual.[3]

Thus, in the developing relationship between an individual and his or her society, socialization involves a dual process. First, it entails the closing off of certain behavioral options. An initially wide range of alternative behaviors is narrowed radically as one is socialized. Second, socialization serves to "make one social" as it opens up and develops the individual, providing him or her with an array of social identities and relationships.

When students of politics adapted socialization notions to their own interests, the Freudian emphasis upon restricting the ideas and behavior of the individual was largely ignored. Students of political socialization have rarely asked: "How does political socialization control the natural antipolitical predispositions of the child?" Students of political socialization have tended to ask instead: "How is the child introduced

[3] George Herbert Mead, *Mind, Self and Society* (Chicago: The University of Chicago Press, 1934).

to his citizenship roles?" "How and when does he develop attachments to the nation? To other political groups?" "How does he come to have particular attitudes toward political authority?" They view political socialization as opening up the world of politics for the individual. It develops the citizen as it opens up a particular social world — the world of political allegiances, political rules and rituals, political policies and personalities, political symbols and behavior.

This emphasis constitutes a break from the use of the term by the early students of culture and personality from whom it was borrowed by early researchers and theorists. This does not mean that political socialization does not include some negative and suppressive aspects. Behaviors that might be detrimental to the stability and well-being of the political community are often inhibited. Acts of disloyalty to the nation, disobedience of laws, and the carrying out of political vendettas are among behavior seen as out of bounds for the "properly socialized citizen." The point here is that more often than not those studying political socialization have focused on the more positive aspect of what is added to the individual through the process.

Another perspective that has influenced research and thinking about political socialization is that of developmental psychology. This influence is most important in those studies that trace the development of political outlooks over the childhood years.[4] Numerous studies have shown how the child's perceptions of the political world undergo considerable development from the period when he or she first enters the elementary school up through the time he or she finishes high school.[5] After identifying patterns of change or development in political orientations the studies have sought to explain them. Several different types of explanations have been advanced. These explanations include the content of messages from the

[4] See, for example, Robert D. Hess and Judith V. Torney, *The Development of Political Attitudes in Children* (Chicago: Aldine, 1967); Fred Greenstein, *Children and Politics* (New Haven: Yale University Press, 1965); and J. Adelson and R. O'Neil, "The Development of Political Thought in Adolescence: The Sense of Community," *Journal of Personality and Social Psychology*, 4 (1966), pp. 296–306.

[5] *Ibid.*

socialization agencies, the generalization from immediate to less immediate relationships (e.g., from family, to school, to political world), and the development of cognitive capacities on the part of the maturing child. Students of political socialization generally view the development of political thinking as closely related to other social learning and thinking.

In the past few years theories of cognitive development have made important contributions toward understanding the development of political thinking. The work of Jean Piaget has been particularly influential.[6] Piaget sees the child's intellectual growth as following a series of stages of cognitive development. From this perspective the child's political outlooks develop as his or her mental capacities develop. Patterns of political learning are tied closely to other types of social learning. The patterns of development are determined in large part by developmental processes innate to the child. Children of age six, seven, or eight have only vague, personalized, and nondiscriminating perceptions of the political world. Only as their cognitive capacities are developed can they begin to come to grips with the complex and often abstract notions and relationships of the political world and their own role in it.

Notions regarding the development of political outlooks are explored more extensively in chapters IV and V. This brief review of two perspectives (the Freudian and the developmental) that influenced thinking about political socialization is presented to suggest the types of things involved in political socialization for the individual.

THE POLITICAL SELF

Political socialization is a developmental process through which the citizen (or potential citizen) matures politically. In this process the individual acquires a complex of information, feelings, and beliefs that help him to comprehend, evaluate,

[6] See, for example, Jean Piaget, *The Moral Judgment of the Child,* trans. Marjorie Gabain (New York: The Free Press, 1965). For a review of research that follows the general framework of Piaget, see Eleanor E. Maccoby, "The Development of Moral Values and Behavior in Childhood," in John Clausen (ed.), *Socialization and Society* (Boston: Little, Brown, 1968), pp. 227–269.

and relate to the political world around him. In many instances his political outlooks are part of his more general social outlooks. Often feelings about political life are related to economic, cultural, and religious views. Trust of political authorities may be closely tied in with a general tendency to trust or not to trust other people. A sense of general dependency upon others to make decisions may be applied to government and the political system. This is not always the case. In some instances an individual may take on political identifications and values that are quite independent of other personal and social outlooks. For example, many Americans develop an identification with a political party that is independent of other social and political outlooks.

Adapting an expression from George Herbert Mead, we say the individual develops a political self, much like he acquires a "social self." [7] The term *political self* refers to the individual's entire complex of orientations regarding the world of politics, including his views toward his own political role. In suggesting the term political self as a shorthand reference to an individual's package of orientations regarding politics, we are borrowing purposefully from Mead's notion of the social self. Through his or her relationships with the social and political world an individual acquires his or her peculiar political self. It is determined in part by the society and its agents, but is also influenced by factors more personal to the individual. As Mead wrote of the social self:

> The self is something which has a development; it is not initially there at birth, but arises in the process of social experience and activity, that is, develops in the given individual as a result of his relations to that process as a whole and to other individuals within the process.[8]

Using this conceptualization we say that political socialization produces for the individual a political self. Three factors give shape to the individual's political self. First, the form and workings of the political system play an important role in determining political orientations. Second, as Mead empha-

[7] Mead, *loc. cit.*
[8] *Ibid.,* p. 135.

sized, the types of experiences and relationships the individual has with other individuals and groups are extremely important. Third, the development of any particular political self will be influenced by the personal needs and capacities of the individual. The political self develops from the interactions among these three factors.

What are the components of the political self? How is it structured? The attitudes, beliefs, and feelings citizens have regarding the political world run a wide gambit. It is difficult to envision a simple classification scheme that can encompass the diversity of political outlooks that can be part of the political self. We suggest that a political self can be characterized by dimensions such as these: It may include a little or a lot of information about the political world. It includes positive, negative, and/or neutral views. Involvement or identification with political symbols ranges from extremely strong to very weak. Individuals may expect anywhere from a great deal to practically nothing from government in services, protection, and assurances.

An individual's political self is likely to consist of the following types of orientations: It is likely to include feelings of nationalism, patriotism, or tribal loyalty. Identification with particular partisan factions, political or social groups, and ideological positions are important components of many political selves. A person's political orientations are likely to include attitudes and evaluations of specific political issues, political personalities, and political events. The political self also involves knowledge regarding political structures and procedures as well as a self-image of rights, responsibilities, and position in the political world.

Not all individuals have developed a political self. The infant is the most common example of a person without a political self. One is not born with an awareness of the political world. Indeed, such an awareness does not develop very fully for a number of years following birth. Adults living in social, geographic, or psychological isolation from most of society may develop only a very rudimentary political self. All societies have persons who exist on their fringe. They have only limited interactions with other citizens. They remain relatively ignorant about their society and have little awareness of what takes place in it. Some awareness of the political world on the part of the individual is a minimal requirement for the development of a political self. Notions about the political world may be correct or incorrect. Feelings about the political system may be positive or negative. Perceptions of the political world may be quite distorted. For the moment our concern is not with the quality of political orientations. Unless a person is at least aware of political objects we cannot speak of his having a political self.

The political self is made. It is not born or innate. *Political maturation* is a process through which a person without an awareness of politics comes to acquire notions concerning the political world and subsequently to develop a complex of political orientations. Political socialization molds and shapes the citizen's relationship to the political community. One aspect of this process can be seen as directing general predispositions picked up in early childhood experiences toward political objects. For example, an orphan child shunted from one institution to another, or from one foster home to another may learn to mistrust adults. He discovers that adults, especially those in positions of authority over him, often behave in capricious ways. The orphan child is also deprived of the security and love characteristic of most parent-child relationships. As a result of these experiences the child may become generally cynical and mistrustful. This general predisposition is not a political orientation. It becomes "political" only when the child encounters political authorities. As an adolescent the orphan may well view the policeman with suspicion. As an adult he may doubt whether government officials are as benevolent and trustworthy as they claim. When his cynicism becomes attached to political objects his general social view becomes part of his political self.

Political socialization also entails experiences that have a direct influence on political outlooks. Early childhood experiences that result in a general tendency to be cynical and mistrustful are not the only things that cause one to distrust government officials. The adult citizen who experiences political mischieviousness and ineptitude on the part of political leaders can come to be distrustful of government, quite independently of early childhood experiences and general propensities toward trusting others.

Acquiring a political self is a corollary to general social maturation. As with other social learning, political learning is gradual and incremental. There is no magic point in childhood or youth when the political self is suddenly acquired. Nor is there any point at which it is fully developed and not subject to alteration. Each citizen's political views result from a lifetime of experiences. Political socialization for the individual entails the gradual molding of the political self — sometimes due to the influence of the deliberate efforts of societal agents and sometimes as a consequence of the more personalized needs and capabilities of the individual.

A convenient way of asking questions about political maturation is to distinguish between different types of political orientations acquired by the citizen. We suggest three very general categories. These categories should not be taken as exhaustive or perfect. They are offered to impose some rough meaningful order to our discussion and to facilitate the posing of important questions. In discussing the orientations an individual has regarding politics we distinguish between the following:

BASIC POLITICAL SENTIMENTS

The basic core of the political self includes a set of basic political attachments and loyalties. These feelings are often very intense and are directed toward the nation or other basic political unit. "I am an American." "I am French." They might also involve attachments to basic political symbols or arrangements. "I am a Communist." "I am a Democrat." In identifying basic loyalties and identifications one also must mention attachments to other significant groupings such as racial categories, religious-ethnic groups, and linguistic or nationality groupings. These may not be political in their own right, but they very often have important implications for more particular political atachments and outlooks.

KNOWLEDGE AND EVALUATIONS OF THE STRUCTURE
AND PROCESSES OF POLITICS

At a slightly less basic level, the political self may be said to include various types of specific knowledge and evaluations of political institutions, roles, and processes. A recognition and appreciation of the role of the presidency and of the legislative body, some understanding of one's rights and duties as a citizen, and assessments of political parties are examples of political outlooks that fall under this general category. Such orientations are important for the citizen in his position as part of a political system.

ORIENTATIONS TO MORE TRANSIENT POLITICAL OBJECTS

The citizen's package of orientations toward politics also includes a less basic and more transient outlook. The citizen reacts to specific policies, programs, personalities, and events. The support of a presidential candidate, favoring or disapproving of particular legislative proposals, and support for or opposition to programs of political change are examples of orientations in this category. They tend to be more in the form of citizen responses to day-to-day political events and propositions.

This scheme allows us to explore questions of political learning by relating them to possible stages in individual development or social maturation. Too often political socialization studies have been limited to listing political socialization agencies on one side of a ledger and a mass of undifferentiated political orientations on the other. This classification scheme allows for more refined hypotheses concerning the relationships between the substance of political orientations, the point in the life cycle where they are acquired, what agencies play a part in their development, and how different types of political orientations are related to each other.

A few illustrations make these several categories more understandable. The earliest and most stable political orientation the individual acquires is his or her identification with a particular political community. Young children the world over seem to know to which nation or other political community they belong. This identification is often accompanied by a strong sense of loyalty toward and positive feelings about that political community. The seven-year-old American child can affirm strongly: "I am an American. America is the best country in the world." He may recognize the American flag and have strong positive feelings about it. At this early point he may have at best only very rudimentary knowledge about American political goals and institutions. A sense of loyalty may exist with very little knowledge about his country's history and its national boundaries. However little substantive content the child's attachment may have at this early age, the sense of identification is quite common. This point was documented in a study of American grade school children:

> The young child's involvement with the political systems begins with a strong positive attachment to the country; the U.S. is seen as ideal and as superior to other countries. This attachment to the country is stable and shows almost no change through elementary school years. This bond is possibly the most basic and essential aspect of socialization into involvement with the political life of the nation. Essentially an emotional tie, it apparently grows from complex psychological and social needs and is exceedingly resistant to change or argument.[9]

As the child is learning loyalty and identification with the political state, he or she develops attachments to other important political symbols. For example, the child may identify with socialism, communism, democracy, or monarchy. As with national identification, at an early age, when the child first becomes aware of these symbols and becomes attached to them, their meanings as ideologies and governmental or social arrangements are not clear. Like the ties to the nation they tend to be emotional and vague.

As the young citizen acquires basic loyalties and identifications with political symbols, he or she also learns to sort people into social categories — linguistic, racial, class, tribal, occupational, geographical. One important aspect of socialization is teaching the child the "social category system" of his or her particular society. Children learn to classify themselves as

[9] Hess and Torney, *op. cit.*, p. 213.

well as others according to certain characteristics. Very often they learn to behave differently toward others depending upon where the others fit in various social categories. The child comes to identify himself or herself as part of particular groups and to adopt behavior appropriate to being part of that particular group rather than another — black rather than white, Jewish rather than gentile, southerner rather than northerner, middle class rather than working class, a French-speaking rather than English-speaking Canadian. Learning the society's social category system and identifying with particular categories are not always in themselves political orientations. These identifications, however, serve as important political reference and interpretation points. One's sense of belonging to one group or category rather than another often is the basis for many important perspectives regarding the political world. For instance, identifying oneself as a black in contemporary American society is very important in the formation of perceptions such as how just and responsive is the political system or the particular political leaders. During the period following the Civil War, identifying oneself as a southerner had very important consequences for important political outlooks such as political party identification and ideas of what the national government should or should not do.

We have stressed here that these basic national, political and social identifications are acquired early in the child's life. They also appear to be among the strongest political outlooks and the most resistant to change in later life. Such orientations as nationalism, group identifications, and partisan attachments seem to have great durability — sometimes even in the face of extensive pressure for change. Partisan attachments in the United States have sometimes continued to endure even after the ideological, sectional, or group rationales upon which they were originally formed have ceased to exist. If we are correct in our assumptions concerning the early acquisition, intensity, and durability of these political and social identities it seems appropriate to hypothesize that they might constitute the core orientations upon which subsequent political orientations are built.

Do such attachments serve to guide later interpretations of
and reactions to more concrete political happenings, such as
choosing between government leaders or public policies? Do
they condition the political roles that the individual will
fashion for himself or herself — whether he or she will be
politically active or passive, an extremist or a moderate, a
strong nationalist or a weak nationalist? The question of how
important these early acquired orientations are for constricting and directing later political life is one of the major issues
in the study of political socialization.

Later in life the individual begins to fill in these vague attachments and identifications with more precise knowledge
and information.[10] These types of political outlooks fit under
the second category of political orientations. Political symbols
come to assume more specific shapes and characteristics.
Democracy ceases to be merely a vague symbol with which the
individual identifies, but one that connotes such things as
citizen participation, competitive elections, and control of
political authorities by constitutional means. The individual
learns how his political world is structured and where he fits
into it. Identifications with political parties and other partisan groups begin to take on ideological and policy meaning.

The political self is never "finalized." The mature citizen is
confronted continuously with new political configurations and
events. He or she is faced with choices about new political
candidates. Different public policies and governmental activities attract his or her attention. Political orientations formed
in the 1930s may be only partially relevant in the 1970s. Attitudes toward specific policies and personalities are, on the
whole, less strongly held than the general political loyalties
and attachments discussed above. The more concrete and specific orientations however, are conditioned — although not
fully determined by — earlier acquired and more intensely
held values. The early acquired political loyalties and identities may provide the citizen in later life with guidelines for
making decisions with respect to day-to-day political events.
The northern, urban, working-class, Catholic, Democrat had

10 See David Easton and Jack Dennis, "The Child's Image of Government," *The Annals*, CCLXI (September 1965), pp. 40–57.

little trouble deciding to vote for Kennedy in 1960 and for Johnson in 1964. The early acquired identifications as working class, Catholic, and Democrat all worked together to condition a favorable response to Kennedy. In other instances the persistence of early acquired identities may lead to considerable tensions. In 1972 the low-income, white supremist, Democratic southerner often found considerable tension between these early acquired identities with the white race, the South, and the Democratic party and the platform and candidate of the national Democratic party. The national Democratic party did not appear consistent with the early acquired identities. Confronted with these inconsistencies many southerners voted for the Republican presidential candidate. Some went so far as to alter their identification with the Democratic party. Others continued to identify themselves as Democrats but saw that attachment in terms of the state party and not the national party. Tensions such as these are fairly common in contemporary American politics, and in most societies where there is important political and social change.

Such phenomena should condition the student of political socialization not to overemphasize the centrality and durability of the basic and early political learning. There are circumstances, and in some points they may be very widespread, in which the outlooks acquired early cease to have much relevance for the individual and his or her relationship to the political world at a later time. The development of the political self may follow a pattern of cumulative development in which early learning conditions later outlooks. However, there may be factors that cause breaks between what is acquired early and what is acquired later.

CHAPTER IV

Political Learning
During Childhood and Adolescence

WHEN DOES POLITICAL LEARNING BEGIN? When, if ever, is it completed? How is political learning paced across the individual's life? Do some types of political learning take place at one stage and other types at other points in the life cycle? Does earlier learning determine political outlooks in later life?

In this chapter we look at political learning during childhood and adolescence. We trace the changing nature of the individual's own "political world" as he or she moves from infancy and early childhood to late childhood and then to adolescence. In Chapter V we look at the adult period. To what extent does the political learning of childhood and adolescence structure or determine adult political outlooks? In Chapter VI we discuss modes of political learning and provide a more comprehensive description of how political learning takes place.

THE IMPORTANCE OF THE PREADULT YEARS

In common folk lore as well as in social theory the childhood years have been recognized as critical for the development of individual personality, social attitudes, and cultural values. In conventional wisdom this idea is expressed in sayings such as: "The child is father to the man." "As the twig is bent so shall the tree grow." The Catholic church has long claimed that if it had influence over the first seven years of the believer's life it could shape the basic values that would guide the remainder of his life. Both Plato and Rousseau, in their concerns for producing good citizens, paid attention to what the child experienced during the early years.[1] Anthropologists and psychoanalytic theorists, concerned with the development of personality and cultural values, have focused on child-rearing practices and early childhood experiences as major determinants of personality and social character.[2] The same emphasis is found in social learning theories [3] and theories stressing cognitive development.[4]

The study of political socialization makes similar assumptions: in childhood we find the roots of adult political life. We share this assumption but add emphatically that political socialization is not limited to childhood or adolescence. It continues throughout life. Some types of political orientations, if not constantly changing, are susceptible to alteration even through adulthood. The political self does not cease developing. Although political learning is continuous, some periods in the life cycle are more important than others in the overall learning process. In many respects the preadult years are those when the most significant political learning takes place.

THE DEVELOPMENT OF POLITICAL OUTLOOKS
OVER THE PREADULT YEARS

To analyze the development of political outlooks during the preadult period, to specify what takes place at what points, and to identify patterns of development, we divide the pre-

[1] See Plato, *The Republic;* and Rousseau, *Emile.*

[2] See, for example, John W. M. Whiting and Irvin L. Child, *Child Training and Personality: A Cross-Cultural Study* (New Haven: Yale University Press, 1953).

[3] See, for example, Neal M. Miller and John Dollard, *Social Learning and Imitation* (New Haven: Yale University Press, 1941); and Albeit Bandura and Richard H. Walters, *Social Learning and Personality Development* (New York: Holt, Rinehart and Winston, 1963).

[4] See, for example, Lawrence Kohlberg, "Stage and Sequence: The Cognitive-Developmental Approach to Socialization," in David A. Goslin (ed.), *Handbook of Socialization Theory and Research* (Chicago: Rand McNally, 1969), pp. 347–480; and Jean Piaget, *The Moral Judgment of the Child* (New York: The Free Press, 1965).

adult years into three periods, suggesting approximate age spans: (1) early childhood (ages five to nine), (2) late childhood (approximately ages nine to thirteen), and (3) adolescence (roughly ages thirteen to eighteen). These age categories are only rough approximations. Human behavior is too complex and social impact too diverse to expect all individuals to follow the same rigid, age-developmental schedule. Nevertheless, these rough age categories fit loosely the findings from studies of American school children and age-development patterns suggested by important theories of individual development. We present a description of how children conceptualize and relate to the political world in each of these three periods and note the changes that take place as we move from one period to the next.

EARLY CHILDHOOD

Some forms of politically relevant learning begin during infancy, as the child comes in contact with the social environment. Two students of political learning report that, "Every piece of evidence indicates that the child's political world begins to take shape well before he even enters elementary school and that it undergoes the most rapid change during these years." [5] Attachment to the nation and feelings toward important symbols such as the flag are among the political outlooks developed during this earliest period.[6] At this point outlooks toward the nation and political symbols are essentially emotional in content. They are in the form of vague feelings and attachments. They lack cognitive or informational content. Early political orientations have been likened to religious feelings.[7]

Attachments to political parties as well as other political identifications are commonly formed by early childhood. In both Fred Greenstein's New Haven study and the study of David Easton and Robert Hess, well over half of the children were able to assert a party attachment by the earliest age

[5] David Easton and Robert D. Hess, "The Child's Political World," *Midwest Journal of Political Science*, VI (1962), pp. 231–232.
[6] *Ibid.*, p. 233.
[7] *Ibid.*, p. 238.

investigated — fourth grade for Greenstein and second grade for Easton and Hess.[8] Like the attachments to the political community, initial partisan outlooks lack cognitive content. Children can say: "I am a Democrat," or "I am a Republican," but cannot say why or what it means. Of the early orientation toward party, Greenstein writes:

> Here, as in children's assessments of the importance of political roles, we find that political feelings, evaluations and attachments form well before the child learns the relevant supporting information. It is not until the fifth grade that the modal child can name at least one party leader, and not until the eighth grade that the children typically name leaders in both parties.[9]

Identifications with social groups also are formed in these early years. The young child has a sense of his social class, his race, and his religion.[10] Racial awareness, for example, appears to form during the preschool years, by ages three to four; "racial orientation" with primitive categories and feelings by ages four to eight; and clear "racial attitudes" by the early grade school years.[10] One study has reported that preschoolers answer questions about race "in a manner which indicated not only awareness of racial differences, but also the use of stereotyped roles." [11] Like other early orientations, these attachments and identifications consist of vague self-definitions that tie one to some people and differentiate one from others. The child learns early that there are blacks and whites, Jews and Catholics, and that he or she is one and not the other.

Basic political attachments are formed at the same time

[8] Fred Greenstein, *Children and Politics* (New Haven: Yale University Press, 1965), p. 21; and Easton and Hess, *op. cit.*, p. 245.

[9] Greenstein, *loc. cit.*

[10] John Harding, Harold Proskansky, Bernard Kutner, and Isador Chein, "Prejudice and Ethnic Relations," in Gardner Lindzey and Elliot Aronson (eds.), *The Handbook of Social Psychology*, 2nd Ed., Vol. 5 (Reading, Mass.: Addison-Wesley, 1969). For a review of literature on early social identifications, see David Sears, "Political Socialization," in Fred I. Greenstein and Nelson Polsby (eds.), *Handbook of Political Science*, Vol. 2 (Reading, Mass.: Addison-Wesley, 1975), pp. 118–119.

[11] Harold W. Stevenson and Edward C. Stewart, "A Developmental Study of Racial Awareness in Young Children," *Child Development*, XXIX (1958), p. 407.

other social attachments are picked up. As the child becomes aware of the political world he or she learns of other social groupings. He discovers that he is rich or poor, part of a special elite or of an oppressed minority group, at the same time he acquires a sense of nationality and identification with a political party. These group identities are often politically important. Through them the individual interprets and relates to the political world.

Along with basic political and social attachments the young child is beginning to develop orientations toward political authorities and roles. As noted in Chapter II, second-, third-, and fourth-graders in the United States view political leaders in highly personalized and indiscriminately positive or benevolent ways. The child seems unable to deal with abstract political relationships and roles. The world of authorities is highly personalized. The policeman, the mayor, and the president are seen as providing personal services and help. The following responses to questions about what various political leaders do illustrate these points: [12]

> The mayor helps people to live in safety. . . . The President is doing a very good job of making people safe. [Fourth-grade girl]
>
> The Board of Aldermen gives us needs so we could live well. [Fourth-grade girl]
>
> The mayor helps everyone to have nice homes and jobs. [Fourth-grade boy]

A study of Australian children reports similar findings.[13] The responses of Gordon, eight:

> *Q:* What kind of thing does the Queen do? . . . What do you hear about her?
> *A:* Oh when she's helping people sometimes.
> *Q:* What people does she help?
> *A:* Poor people.
> *Q:* How does she do that?
> *A:* Gives them jewels and that. . . .
> *Q:* What do you think of the Prime Minister?

[12] Greenstein, *op. cit.*

[13] R. W. Connell, *The Child's Construction of Politics* (Melbourne: Melbourne University Press, 1971), p. 26.

A: He's very kind to people.
Q: What does he do for people?
A: Helps them.
Q: How does he do that?
A: Someone's dying well he asks some famous doctors or some doctors with good medicine to fix them. . . .
Q: What would a bad Prime Minister do?
A: If someone was badly injured, they wouldn't help them.

The president and others in authority are seen also as persons with power, as people of importance. Easton and Dennis report the following responses of an eight-year-old to questions of the role of the president: [14]

I: What does the President do?
A: He runs the country, he decides the decisions that he should try to get out of and he goes to meetings and he tries to make peace and things like that. . . .
I: When you say he runs the country, what do you mean?
A: Well, he's just about the boss of everything.

Easton and Dennis find that the president is a visible figure to most young children. He is the major figure through which they develop their early relationships and conceptions of the political world. He is seen as both powerful and benevolent. He can cause things to get done and he does good things.

Political learning is underway by early childhood. The young child has become aware of some political figures. In the United States the president looms large. Orientations, however, consist largely of feelings or affects. There is little understanding of government or political ideologies. Political authorities are seen in predominantly personal and benevolent ways.

LATE CHILDHOOD

During late childhood, between age nine and thirteen, political outlooks take on new character. Changes in political perceptions between the early childhood period and the end of late childhood are so great that for some scholars this is the

14 David Easton and Jack Dennis, *Children in the Political System* (New York: McGraw-Hill, 1969), p. 145.

most important period for political learning.[15] By age ten or eleven children begin to move away from the highly personal and emotional perceptions and to comprehend more abstract ideas and relationships. Where younger children can do little more than identify political leaders, especially the president, as powerful and benevolent, older children show a greater capacity to understand and identify certain tasks that go along with particular political roles. During this period information and cognitive content are added to the vague feelings and identifications acquired earlier.

One study of political socialization that examined changes in boys from age ten to fourteen stressed the accomplishment in political reasoning that had occurred by the pre- and early-adolescent period. The boys were asked why the president is reasonable most of the time. The older boys were able to respond that unreasonable behavior would be punished: ". . . we would not re-elect him. Congress would not pass his bills, he would not be voted money to run the government, he might be impeached." Such formulations were beyond the capacity of the younger boys. The older boys indicated a more complicated and sensitive understanding of the restraints within which the president operates.[16]

Along with a growing capacity to differentiate and perceive impersonal roles, an increase in political information or knowledge occurs in the transition from age nine to thirteen. This growth in knowledge among a sample of grammar school children is shown in Table IV.1. Children in the lower grades know the name of the president and mayor, but few know much about their roles and duties. By grades seven and eight (twelve and thirteen years of age), the number of children able to provide reasonable answers about political roles had increased substantially. With greater cognitive capacity in late childhood children also are able to distinguish between political roles and the individuals that fill them. For young children the presidency and the incumbent president tend to be one

[15] Easton and Hess, *op. cit.*, pp. 237–238.

[16] Roberta Sigel, "Political Socialization: Some Reflections on Current Approaches and Conceptualizations," Unpublished paper presented at the Meetings of the American Political Science Association, New York, September 1966, p. 8.

TABLE IV.1 *"Reasonably Accurate" Responses to Selected Political Information Items: Arranged by School Year*

Information Asked	School Grade				
	4th	*5th*	*6th*	*7th*	*8th*
President's name	96%	97%	90%	99%	100%
Mayor's name	90	97	89	99	97
President's duties	23	33	44	65	66
Mayor's duties	35	42	50	66	67
Governor's duties	8	12	23	36	43
Role of state legislature	5	5	9	24	37
Number of cases	111	118	115	135	180

Source: Fred I. Greenstein, "The Benevolent Leader: Children's Images of Political Authority," *American Political Science Review* LIV (1960), p. 937. Reprinted by permission of the American Political Science Association.

Interpretation: The higher the grade the more accurate the knowledge. These data show a consistent development of political knowledge during the five-grade span, emphasizing the amount of political learning that takes place during the preadolescent years.

and the same. Children in late childhood can make distinctions between the acts of a particular president and the office itself.

The greatest leap in the child's understanding of the political world seems to occur between ages eleven and thirteen. Only then do children acquire the elementary capacity to understand political and social relationships. By the end of childhood children's political ideas have developed from considerable ignorance of the geographic, social, and political world around them to an outlook that is not very different from the perceptions and understanding of mature adults.

ADOLESCENCE

Adolescence is a period of major change and general development — physically, psychologically, and socially.[17] Adolescents are learning to be adults — acquiring social skills, forming internal standards of judgment and conduct, and developing participatory skills. Adolescence is a period of in-

[17] For a collection of articles on adolescence, see Jerome Kogan and Robert Coles (eds.), *12 to 16 Early Adolescence* (New York: Norton, 1971).

creasing freedom from the influence of parents. There is less association with parents and a decrease in the importance of parental evaluations. Peers become increasingly important.

What happens with respect to political learning during this period? By the early teens the child is likely to have acquired major components of a mature political self. Basic political attachments and identifications are well established. The strong emotional feelings regarding political institutions, symbols, and authorities have been supplemented with knowledge of more specific roles and functions. By early adolescence much of the political world has been mapped out. This does not mean, however, that no development takes place during adolescence. The ability of the child to understand and to think about politics continues to grow during adolescence. The changes may not be as startling as those that take place between early childhood and late childhood, but they are important. To some extent they involve refinements and advancements in the important developments of late childhood.

Joseph Adelson has investigated the shifts in the character of political thinking from age twelve to eighteen. On the basis of interviews with 450 adolescents in the United States, West Germany, and Great Britain, he suggests three basic types of shifts in political thinking during adolescence: (1) change in cognitive mode, (2) a sharp decline in authoritarian views of the political system, and (3) achievement of a capacity for ideological thinking.[18] Adelson makes two general points about the developments he finds over the adolescent years.

First, the developments that take place between age eleven and eighteen seem to be due primarily to age and maturation. Although there were some national differences in political thinking, these differences were not nearly as strong as age affects. "A twelve-year-old German youngster's ideas of politics are closer to those of a twelve-year-old American than to those of his fifteen-year-old brother." [19] Adelson reports that sex, intelligence, and social class do not count for much in the growth of political conceptualization. Bright adolescents can

[18] Joseph Adelson, "The Political Imagination of the Young Adolescent," in Kogan and Coles, *Ibid.*
[19] *Ibid.*, p. 108.

deal with abstractions a little earlier, and upper middle-class youngsters are somewhat less authoritarian than those from lower classes, but these differences are minor. What counts most heavily is *age*.

Second, the most important changes take place in the transition from early to middle adolescence. On the threshold of adolescence, at age twelve or thirteen, the child adheres to tangible, concrete events and people in his or her view of the political world. By age fifteen or sixteen, the adolescent can deal with abstractions in relating to his or her society or community and in conceptualizing general principles. At twelve or thirteen the child does not have a sense of community, that is, in understanding concepts such as authority, rights, liberty, equity, and representation. By age fifteen he does. In early adolescence the child, in thinking about politics, has no sense of history and the future. As he reaches middle adolescence he begins to look beyond the short-run impact to long-term effects; his time perspective is enlarged.[20]

During this time the quality of thought becomes more complex. The youngster by midadolescence acquires an increased grasp of human complexities and improved modes of reasoning. He or she acquires a capacity for hypothesis-deductive thinking and a greater ability to look at alternative choices in terms of cost-benefit analysis and conditional explanations ("if . . . then" and "it depends upon"). These changes can be illustrated by comparing responses to the question of the purpose of laws: [21]

(twelve- and thirteen-year-olds)
They do it, like in schools, so that people don't get hurt.
If we had no laws, people could go around killing people.
So people don't steal or kill.

(fourteen- and fifteen-year-olds)
To ensure safety and enforce the government.
To limit what people can do.
They are basically guidelines for people. I mean, like this is wrong and this is right and to help them understand.

20 *Ibid.*, pp. 110–111.
21 *Ibid.*, p. 108.

The twelve- and thirteen-year-olds respond in terms of concrete examples — stealing, killing, and so on. Adolescents two years older use more abstract conceptualization, often backed up with concrete examples.

Adelson also finds a decrease in authoritarianism. He found an ingenuous belief in the good and justice of authority among the youngest adolescents. "Young adolescents will not spontaneously imagine that authority might be capricious, arbitrary, or mistaken." [22] They show a tendency to support law, even when they are not altogether clear about its purpose. They express the feeling that it is a duty to obey laws. Toward government and law they are trusting, uncritical, acquiescent. These tendencies change as the youths move through adolescence.

During adolescence there is an increase in the amount and quality of political knowledge, with an understanding of political phenomena instead of just factual knowledge. The period is also marked by increased interest in political affairs. As they move through adolescence the youths become more likely to follow political events, develop a more active identification with a political party, and participate in political groups and electoral activities. In short, they begin to take on more "adult" political interests and involvements.[23]

Important aspects of political maturation continue through later adolescence, but for the most part developments during these later years involve the crystallization and internalization of patterns established earlier. In their study of the growth of political ideas, Adelson and Robert O'Neil summarize the changes from late childhood to late adolescence as follows:[24]

>   *Eleven-year-olds:* We might say that the 11-year-old has not achieved the capacity for formal operations. His thinking is concrete, ego-centric, tied to the present; he is unable to envision long-range social consequences; he cannot comfortably

[22] *Ibid.,* p. 117.

[23] See Herbert H. Hyman, *Political Socialization* (New York: The Free Press, 1959), pp. 51–68, for a review of this literature.

[24] Joseph Adelson and Robert P. O'Neil, "Growth of Political Ideas in Adolescence: The Sense of Community," *Journal of Personality and Social Psychology,* IV (1966), pp. 305–306.

reason from premises; he has not attained hypothetico-deductive modes of analysis.

Thirteen-year-olds: The 13-year-old has achieved these capacities some (much?) of the time, but is unable to display them with any consistent effectiveness.

Fifteen-year-olds The 15-year-old has an assured grasp of formal thought. He neither hesitates nor falters in dealing with the abstract.

Eighteen-year-olds: Taking our data as a whole we usually find only moderate differences between 15 and 18. . . . The 18-year-old is, in other words, the 15-year-old, only more so. He knows more; he speaks from a more extended apperceptive mass; he is more facile; he can elaborate his ideas more fluently. Above all, he is more philosophical, more ideological in his perspective on the political order.

GENERAL PATTERNS IN PREADULT POLITICAL LEARNING

We have looked at preadult political learning by describing political orientations in three rough age groupings. At this point we offer some generalizations to describe developments over the preadult period. Then we consider the question of whether these generalizations are applicable to different population groups and over different periods.

Although patterns of human development are complex and variable, and research findings are not always consistent, the following generalizations can be made about the content and development of preadult political learning, at least for contemporary American society:

1. Political learning begins early and continues through early childhood, late childhood, and adolescence.

2. Different types of political learning take place at different points over the preadult years.

3. Basic attachments and identifications — those orientations we identified in Chapter III as the core components of the political self — are among the first political outlooks to be acquired.

4. Early orientations toward political authorities seem to be indiscriminately positive and benevolent. They become less so as the child moves through late childhood and into adolescence.

5. Early conceptions of politics and government are highly personalized. The government, the president, the mayor, and so on are understood initially in personal terms. This personalization fades and is replaced by more abstract perceptions by late childhood and early adolescence.

6. Affective orientations, or feelings about political objects, seem to be acquired before information or knowledge. One has feelings about the nation and the president (usually positive feelings) before one has much understanding of what they are.

7. During late childhood the child acquires information and knowledge about the political world. He or she begins to distinguish between different political roles and to acquire the basic factual information needed to map out the political world.

8. During adolescence the individual increases his or her capacity to deal with abstractions, and to engage in ideological thinking and ends-means analysis. He or she becomes more interested in following political events and more involved in partisan and electoral politics.

9. Because different types of political learning occur at different points over the preadult years it is difficult to specify any particular period as the most important or crucial point. If one places importance on the ability of the maturing citizen to understand political roles and relationships, the end of late childhood and early adolescence might be regarded as most significant — roughly the period between ages eleven and fifteen.

10. Political learning seems to coincide with other types of social learning. Political identities are formed during the same period when other social identities are acquired. The development of political thinking follows the capacity of the individual to handle abstractions and engage in the types of thinking necessary for understanding social and political relationships.

11. By the end of the preadult years the political self is well developed. Most of the basic orientations and knowledge about the political world, as well as the capacity to understand political relationships, are acquired or developed as far as they are likely to be.

ARE THESE GENERAL PATTERNS APPLICABLE TO ALL CHILDREN?

To what extent are the age-developmental patterns outlined above descriptive of childhood political learning for different types of childen? Do children from different racial and ethnic groupings and from different social class backgrounds tend to share the same types of political outlooks and develop political orientations according to the same patterns? Are there different developmental patterns for boys and girls? If there are differences in content and developmental patterns, when and how are such differences apparent?

One important finding of the early studies of childhood political socialization was the highly positive and indiscriminately benevolent feelings that young children have toward the nation, its basic symbols, and toward important authority figures. A wide range of studies suggests that this is a universal phenomenon. During the early childhood years blacks, Chicanos, and lower class children in the United States share the idealization of political authorities. To the extent that studies have been made elsewhere the same pattern holds true outside the United States. There is also a universal tendency for positive outlooks toward political authorities to diminish as the child reaches late childhood or early adolescence.[25]

Following that initial period of universal positive outlooks, differences among various subgroups begin to appear. There are variations in the rate of political maturity and in the content of political outlooks. Seven- and eight-year-old blacks in contemporary America share positive opinions of the president and the police. Older black youths, however, feel less positive about political authorities such as the police than their white counterparts.[26] Blacks and whites may share the same positive feelings in early childhood. Both experience the erosion of positive, benevolent outlooks as they get older, but the decrease among blacks is markedly steeper than that among whites. The same pattern of divergence appears among Chicanos and "Anglos" in the latter part of the preadult years.[27]

The pattern of common positive outlooks during the early

[25] See Sears, *op. cit.*, p. 105.

[26] See Edward Greenberg, "Orientations of Black and White Children to Political Authority," *Social Science Quarterly*, 51 (1970), pp. 934–943.

[27] See F. Chris Garcia, *Political Socialization of Chicano Children* (New York: Praeger, 1973).

childhood years and more diverse positions later on suggests there may be some common characteristics of early childhood, related either to individual developmental processes or to the impact of certain socializing agents or messages, which lead to indiscriminately positive outlooks toward political authorities and symbols. By late childhood or early adolescence, however, particular outlooks reflect the picture of the political world one has from one's position as a young black, a young Chicano, or a middle-class white. The divergences during this latter period also seem more consistent with the perspectives of the adults making up the various population groupings. The early positive orientations may be unrelated to concrete perceptions and evaluations of the political world, but more reflective of the particular needs of the young child and his ability to perceive and think about the political world.

Social class and group differences are apparent with respect to other types of early political outlooks and the development of political thinking. At an early age young blacks tend to feel less efficacious and powerful in political life than their white contemporaries.[28] When compared to middle-class children, lower class children, across the various age categories, lag behind in reaching political maturity. They persist longer in the idealized and benevolent images of political authorities, and they maintain until later the perception of law as absolute, unchanging, and inherently just.[29] Robert Hess and Judith Torney found that children from higher status backgrounds were more likely to engage in political discussions with parents and friends, and that these social class differences were apparent as early as the third and fourth grades.[30]

Sex also seems to make a difference in the content and processes of political learning during childhood. Among third- to eighth-graders, girls have been found to have a more "immature" picture of the president and the policeman than boys of the same age. Girls also have tended to hold on to the

[28] Sears, *op. cit.,* p. 109.

[29] Robert Weissberg, *Political Learning, Political Choice and Democratic Citizenship* (Englewood Cliffs, N.J.: Prentice-Hall, 1974), p. 95–106.

[30] Robert Hess and Judith Torney, *The Development of Political Attitudes in Children* (Chicago: Aldine, 1967), p. 178.

more idealized and personalized image of political authorities longer than boys.[31] Starting as early as the fourth grade, boys have been found to be better informed about political matters than girls.[32] They are also more likely to get involved in political campaign activities. Participation in campaign-type activities increases markedly for both sexes between the third and eighth grades, but at each grade level boys were more active than girls. Among high school seniors, boys have been found to "exhibit a greater sense of capacity to manipulate the political environment." [33]

These childhood and adolescent sex differences correspond closely to the image of such differences among adults. It is interesting to note how early these patterns become established. The fact that they are apparent so early in life certainly has meaning for the difficulty in bringing about change in sex roles among adults and suggests where efforts for change will have to begin.

DO THE POSITIVE FEELINGS TOWARD AUTHORITY HOLD OVER TIME?

Since the studies of the early 1960s first reported the idealization of political authority among American school children, questions have been raised concerning the validity of the findings and the reasons behind the positive outlooks. One point that received considerable attention is the suggestion that the positive feelings resulted from the fact that these first studies were conducted during the Eisenhower and Kennedy presidencies. These were years when the incumbent presidents were held in high personal esteem and in which there were few substantial conflicts or intense partisan divisions. What would happen, it was often asked, if similar questions were posed in a period when the incumbent president was not personally esteemed and/or in a period of considerable conflict and tension?

Historical events have provided just such a situation. Students of political behavior have begun to reinvestigate this

31 *Ibid.,* pp. 205–212.
32 Greenstein, *op. cit.,* p. 117.
33 Weissberg, *op. cit.,* p. 117.

issue. The intense conflicts of the late 1960s and early 1970s, the credibility problems that beset the latter years of the Johnson administration, the Watergate scandals that led to the resignation of President Nixon, and the substantial decrease in political trust among adult citizens have provided a setting for a reinvestigation of the benevolent leader notion.

Do children and adolescents continue to express indiscriminately benevolent orientations toward the president in the wake of almost a decade of governmental and presidential crises? Or have preadults followed the adult citizenry toward more cynical and less benevolent feelings toward government and the president, in particular. Several studies of childhood and adolescent outlooks in the early 1970s are available now.[34] Although the findings are neither conclusive nor consistent at this point, and it is too early to speculate on the long-range impact of these events on either contemporary or future young people, some tentative points can be made.

Taken as whole the evidence suggests that over the past few years preadults have become less likely to express the strongly positive and benevolent feelings toward the president than those found in studies of the early 1960s. Studies, some using the same items to measure feelings toward the president, have found a substantial decrease in the frequency of positive response to the president. These findings offer support for the notion that preadult attitudes toward central authorities such as the president are conditioned by the political situation. Given a popular president with a good personal image and a peaceful and positive political climate, children tend to have positive outlooks toward the president. During a period in which the president is not highly regarded and there is a less positive political setting, childhood outlooks toward the president are less likely to be so indiscriminately positive.

Two studies suggest some important qualifications to the general findings of decrease in positive effect. A recent study by Marjorie Hershey and David Hill used items from the

[34] See, for example, F. Christopher F. Arterton, "The Impact of Watergate on Children's Attitudes Toward Political Authority," *Political Science Quarterly* (June 1974), pp. 269–288; Majorie Randon Hershey and David B. Hill, "Watergate and Preadults' Attitudes Toward the President," *American Journal of Political Science* (November 1975), pp. 703–726.

Easton-Hess investigation of the early 1960s to investigate childhood outlooks of the early 1970s.[35] They found an overall decrease in positive regard for the president, but they found an age-related pattern in this drop-off that seems to have relevance for understanding how and why political outlooks develop in childhood. Questions were administered to a sample of second-, fourth-, sixth-, eighth-, tenth-, and twelfth-graders in Florida. Using the same items Easton and Hess employed, they make explicit age comparisons with the findings from the early 1960s. Responses to a key question on presidential responsiveness for 1961–62 and for 1973–74 studies are presented in Table IV.2.

In both the 1960s and 1970s there is an age-related decline in positive responses. The tendency to idealize presidential authority decreases as the children become older. Sixth- and eighth-graders in the post-Watergate study are decidely less likely to give positive responses than their grade counterparts in the early 1960s. The decrease in positive responses continues through the high school years. These findings suggest that outlooks toward presidential authority may well have been influenced by Watergate and other political events of the past decade.

However, a somewhat different picture appears among the second- and fourth-graders. Unlike the big change among older children the percentage of second- and fourth-graders who respond by saying the president cares a lot does not decrease between the two studies. In fact, the tendency to give the most positive response increases somewhat, a sharp contrast to the negative movement among the older children. For all age groups there is a tendency for more of the children to choose the most negative response in the post-Watergate years than was true in the early sixties. However, the proportion of "only a little" responses does not become particularly high until after the fourth grade.

The tendency toward idealization of the president remains high among the younger children. They seem to have been less

---

[35] Marjorie Randon Hershey and David B. Hill, "Watergate and the Benevolent Leader," A paper presented at the 33rd Annual Meeting of the Midwest Political Science Association, May 1–3, 1975, Chicago, Illinois.

TABLE IV.2 *Change in Perceived Presidential Responsiveness*

				Grade (Years)			
I. Easton-Hess Results (1961–62)	2 (7)	4 (9)	6 (11)	8 (13)	10 (15)	12 (17)
The president cares [a] A lot	75.2%	56.4%	46.3%	43.1%		
Some	19.6	36.3	42.3	43.0		
A little	5.1	7.2	11.4	13.9		
	99.9%	99.9%	100.0%	100.0%		
$N =$	1,639	1,738	1,744	1,686		
Gamma = .32						
II. 1973–74 Results						
The president cares A lot	78.8%	64.5%	32.4%	27.6%	21.5%	16.3%
Some	10.2	14.9	29.3	34.2	28.3	33.9
Only a little	11.0	20.5	38.3	38.2	50.2	49.8
	100.0%	99.9%	100.0%	100.0%	100.0%	100.0%
$N =$	283	375	355	351	307	313
Gamma = .45						

Source: Marjorie Randon Hershey and David B. Hill, "Watergate and the Benevolent Leader," a paper presented at the 33rd Annual Meeting of the Midwest Political Science Association, May 1–3, 1975, Chicago, Illinois, p. 8. Reprinted by permission of the authors and the Midwest Political Science Association.

[a] The question reads: "Which do you think is the most true? Choose one. If you write to the president, he cares (a lot, some, a little) what you think." Source for the 1961–62 data: David Easton and Jack Dennis, *Children in the Political System* (New York: McGraw-Hill, 1969), p. 185 (Table 8–5); and Robert D. Hess and Judith V. Torney, *The Development of Political Attitudes in Children* (Chicago: Aldine, 1967), p. 40 (Table 8).

influenced by Watergate and other presidential and governmental events of the past decade than were the older children.
These findings take on particular meaning because they fit
the findings with respect to group differences discussed above.
The positive outlooks of early childhood were found to be
unrelated to racial and ethnic differences. Racial and ethnic
differences with respect to government and regard for authorities were evident only among older children. Both of
these patterns also fit the general notion of changes between
early and late childhood with respect to the capacity of the
child to perceive the political world and to cope with political knowledge and relationships. Older children are more
likely than the younger children to heed what takes place in
the political world and to be influenced by it.

Another type of qualification to the decreased tendency to
idealize presidential authority among children is suggested by
Fred Greenstein in two recent studies. On the bases of interviews with children during the late 1960s and early 1970s
Greenstein found that the first-term Nixon counterparts of the
children of the Eisenhower-Kennedy era, "were extraordi-
narily positive in their spontaneous descriptions of the President." [36] He suggests that "much of the preponderance of
favorable over unfavorable effect reflects positive assumptions
about the leadership *role* and its importance to society. Children appear able – in a wholly unself-conscious way – to distinguish between roles and the individuals who fill them." [37]
In a slightly later study Greenstein found that responses of
seventh-graders in the midst of the negative publicity surrounding Watergate (mid-1973) indicate that negative judgments were directed to the performance of the incumbent
president and not to the presidential role. This was true
even when the children made references to bribery, corrup-
tion, and impeachment in responses to open-ended questions.
Manifestation of respect for the presidency itself continues.
The children interviewed in the midst of the Watergate crisis

[36] Fred Greenstein, "The Benevolent Leader Revisited: Children's
Images of Political Leaders in Three Democracies," *American Political
Science Review* (December 1975), p. 1385.
[37] *Ibid.*, p. 1390.

showed a slight decline in idealization of the president in spite of the continuation of benevolent leader imagery. Greenstein concludes that, "although these children (post-Watergate period) still idealized the presidential role in the abstract, they were prepared to punish a presidential malefactor." [38]

UNDERSTANDING PATTERNS OF PREADULT POLITICAL LEARNING

We have described the development of political thinking and the acquisition of political outlooks over the preadult years. We have identified several patterns of development and asked whether these patterns hold for various types of children and over differing political climates. How can we account for, or understand, these patterns. Why do young children tend to have such positive outlooks toward political authority? Why is this perspective universal, and not conditioned by social position or political setting? What factors account for the rapid increase in political knowledge and the ability to deal with political relationships during late childhood? Why is it only during early adolescence that one becomes capable of ideological and analytical thinking about politics? Why are older children more influenced by events such as Watergate and by their position as part of various social, economic, ethnic, and racial groupings? Are these patterns explainable by internally motivated processes of maturation? By the lessons and perspectives passed on by various agents of socialization? By the growth of capacity to deal with the social and political environment? Or by combinations of all of these?

These important questions are posed, but not answered by the description of developments over the age periods. Three different types of theories of social and personal development have been advanced for dealing with questions such as these: (1) psychodynamic theories, (2) social learning theories, and (3) cognitive-developmental theories. These three types of theory approach the development of the political self in different ways. Each has some utility in understanding political socialization.

[38] *Ibid.,* p. 1397.

PSYCHODYNAMIC THEORIES

This approach to individual development has been influenced by Freudian psychoanalytic conceptualizations. The emphasis is upon stages of maturation that are internal to the individual. Experiences during infancy and very early childhood are crucial in shaping the needs and personality dynamics of the individual. The earliest experiences are depicted as very intense. They leave a deep imprint upon the developing personality. In both conscious and unconscious ways, the early formed internal needs determine how the child and later the adult will respond to objective events and other stimuli.

From this perspective the individual adopts outlooks toward the political world as a means of satisfying his or her own personal needs and personality dynamics. One adopts particular orientations toward political authorities on the basis of one's own needs and personal experiences. One goes into politics because one has a "need" for power. One is acquiescent to political authorities because one has a "need" to submit to the domination of others. This approach has been proposed to explain the indiscriminately positive outlooks young children have toward political authorities. Two different hypotheses of the psychodynamic type have been advanced. One suggests that the positive orientations toward the president and other authority figures result from the transference of feelings developed toward the father onto other authority figures. On the basis of early, immediate, and personal relationships with his or her father, the child develops positive and benevolent feelings toward him. Sensing something analogous between the relationship with the father and more distant authorities the child transfers the positive feelings toward the father to other authority figures as he or she becomes aware of them. This construction was suggested by Greenstein and by Easton and Hess as possible explanations for the early acquired, positive outlooks toward authority figures.[39]

Another psychodynamic type of explanation of this positive

[39] See Greenstein, *Children and Politics op. cit.*, pp. 46–52; and Easton and Hess, *op. cit.*

orientation is the *vulnerability hypothesis.* This hypothesis suggests that when confronted with the awesome powers of the presidency the young child feels quite vulnerable. As a means of dealing with the anxieties created by this vulnerability he or she comes to believe that the president will use that power in a helpful and protective way. In both of these interpretations the particular orientations toward the president are motivated by personal relationships and needs.

SOCIAL-LEARNING THEORIES

Social-learning theory precedes from the opposite starting point. It stresses the stimuli the individual receives from his or her environment and the reinforcement for particular outlooks provided in that environment. The messages the individual receives from the environment are the crucial factors in determining the outlooks the individual will adopt.

Dealing with the causes of the positive outlooks toward authorities among young children, a social-learning model would look at the messages the young child receives from parents, teachers, and the media concerning authority figures. The young child may develop positive-benevolent outlooks toward the policeman because his parents and teachers stress that the policeman is on the corner to help him get across the street safely. He is admonished both at home and at school to obey the policeman because in that way he will be protected and aided. The same message may also be communicated to the young child through children's books, which portray the policeman as one of several individuals there to help and protect him. The same messages may be conveyed to the young child with respect to other authority figures. Listen to the teacher. She is there to help you learn. Obey the law and government; they are there to help us get along with each other in peace and harmony and provide us with things we cannot take care of on our own.

COGNITIVE-DEVELOPMENTAL THEORIES

The distinctions between the psychodynamic model and the social-learning model are rather clear-cut. The former sees particular attitudes, orientations, and behavior formed in response to inner needs, the latter as a response to stimuli in the environment. The cognitive-developmental model falls somewhere in between. It emphasizes the interaction between the environment and the developing capacity of the individual to deal with the environment. How the maturing individual responds and understands the things he experiences in the environment depends in large measure on the advancement of his or her basic thinking capacity. The cognitive capacity of the individual develops through a series of different stages. These different stages involve qualitatively distinct modes of thinking. The ways in which the individual experiences, categorizes, and relates to objects in the environment change as he or she moves from infancy, to early childhood, to late childhood and adolescence. Different cognitive capacities are closely, but not rigidly, related to age sequences. Older children whose cognitive capacity is further advanced are in a position to understand and think about politics in a manner quite different from younger children.

From this perspective the highly positive orientations toward authorities and the later decline in such outlooks are related to the varied age-related ability of the individual to perceive authorities and their relationships with them. The thinking of the young child is egocentric. It is absolutist rather than relative. It cannot deal with abstractions such as institutions and political roles. These factors condition the child to experience authority during the early days in positive, benevolent, and highly personalized terms.

Each of these approaches offers something to an understanding of early political outlooks. The early idealization and personalization of authority may result from the consistent impact of each of these factors. The psychological needs of the young child, his or her particular capacity to deal with political ideas and relationships, and the messages he or she receives about the political world may all work together to the same end — an indiscriminately positive, benevolent, and highly personalized perspective. What about other types of political learning, and political learning at other points in the life cycle? It would seem that different approaches may be more or less useful in explaining different types of development.

Changes in the understanding of political roles and relationships that take place between early childhood and late childhood and midadolescence (the periods in which there is the greatest development in knowledge and thinking about politics) can be understood best by the cognitive-developmental model. The types of changes outlined above seem to follow rather closely the types of developmental stages and modes of thinking suggested by cognitive-developmental theorists such as Jean Piaget, Lawrence Kohlberg, and Joseph Adelson. Those students of political socialization who have been most concerned with the development of political thinking and the capacity for ideology, such as Adelson and Richard Merelman, use cognitive-developmental notions to understand these types of significant developments in political maturation.[40]

Other types of political learning can be explained better by the social learning type of explanations. The formation and changes of opinions and preferences during adulthood, and even some types of political learning during adolescence are influenced by environmental stimuli and reinforcement rather than through general developments of cognitive capacity and political thinking. The recent decrease in trust and respect for government and the president among adult Americans cannot be explained very well be psychodynamic or cognitive-developmental models. Such change can be understood best by a model that stresses stimuli in the environment.

[40] Richard M. Merelman, "The Development of Political Ideology: A Framework for the Analysis of Political Socialization," *American Political Science Review*, LXIII (1969), pp. 750–767.

CHAPTER V

Age and the Political Self: The Adult Years

THE IMPACT OF EARLY POLITICAL SOCIALIZATION

In Chapter IV we discussed political socialization during childhood and adolescence. We stressed that much political learning is accomplished during those years. In this chapter we turn to political socialization in the adult years. In moving to the adult years two questions must be considered. First, what impact does the considerable political learning of the early years have upon adult political outlooks? Does the early learning shape adult political life? Or are adult political outlooks formed independently of what was learned during childhood and youth? Second, what types of political learning, if any, take place during the adult years? Are some types of orientations more or less likely to be formed or altered during the adult period? What types of experiences contribute to alterations or developments in the political self during this later period?

The relevancy of early political socialization for adult life is one of the most important questions confronting students of political socialization. The proposition that early political learning is crucial in determining adult political outlooks and behavior has been a core assumption in most of the thinking and research on the subject. It has been the major motivation behind the studies of childhood political learning that have appeared over the past decade or two. If childhood learning is not important for adult political life there is little reason for the student of politics to devote much attention to the subject.

Two studies that deal with the consequences of political socialization base their arguments on the assumption that early learning has important consequences for later political life. The study by David Easton and Jack Dennis, which we reviewed in Chapter II, focuses upon the consequences of political socialization patterns for the persistence of political systems.[1] The authors argue that the positive and supportive orientations toward the system and its symbols established during the early childhood years contribute to the diffuse support for the existing political system among adults. Without such early formed attachments the persistence of political systems would be extremely problematic. Robert Weissberg analyzes the role of early political socialization in determining the quality of participation and the adherence to democratic values among American citizens.[2] He, too, bases his argument on the proposition that adult orientations are determined, in large measure, by the political orientations acquired in childhood. The early acquisition of many important political orientations and their persistence throughout life severely limit the effective choices open to adult citizens.[3]

> If politics involves a choice of alternatives among different ways of organizing and governing political life, and each individual begins life with the full array of choices before him, we can readily see that by adolescence most Americans have narrowed down the range of political alternatives.

Most students of political socialization have accepted the proposition that what happens during the preadult years has consequences for adult political outlooks and behavior. In recent years, however, some scholars have questioned just how crucial the early years are. Some have argued that the early acquired political outlooks do not always appear to be very

[1] David Easton and Jack Dennis, *Children in the Political System: Origins of Political Legitimacy* (New York: McGraw-Hill, 1969).

[2] Robert Weissberg. *Political Learning, Political Choice and Democratic Citizenship* (Englewood Cliffs, N.J.: Prentice-Hall, 1974).

[3] *Ibid.,* pp. 58–59.

closely associated with the political choices made during the adult years.[4] Some have suggested that events and experiences more contemporaneous to adult political choices may have more bearing on those choices than the political learning of childhood. Gabriel Almond and Sidney Verba argue:[5]

> Early socialization experiences significantly affect an individual's basic personality predispositions and may therefore affect his political behavior, but numerous other factors intervene between these earliest experiences and later political behavior that greatly inhibit the impact of the former on the latter. Such basic dimensions of political behavior as the degree of activity or involvement in politics or the individual's partisan affiliation seem to be best explained in terms of later experiences.

There is very little research that has adequately investigated the persistence of given political outlooks for given individuals over the entire life span. Such analysis would require longitudinal analysis, following changes and stability in political outlooks for given individuals over a span of several decades. The question of how important early political learning is for determining adult political outlooks and behavior, thus, remains unresolved.

There are many different arguments as to when the most significant political learning takes place. Three different models can be identified.[6] They are discussed here to make clearer the issues and controversies surrounding the question of the relationship between early political learning and adult political life. The three are (1) the primacy model, (2) the recency model, and (3) the intermediate-period model. Each of these models asserts the significance of a different period in the life cycle for political learning. The different emphases can be seen clearly by comparing the three diagrams presented in Figure V.1.

[4] See Donald D. Searing, Joel J. Schwartz, and Allen E. Lind, "The Structuring Principle: Political Socialization and Belief Systems," *American Political Science Review*, 67 (June 1973), pp. 415–432.

[5] Gabriel A. Almond and Sidney Verba, *The Civic Culture* (Princeton: Princeton University Press, 1963), p. 324.

[6] Our argument concerning these three models has been influenced by the discussion of these issues by Weissberg, *op. cit.*, pp. 23–31.

FIGURE V.1 *Relevance of Political Learning for Adult Political Attitudes and Behaviors*

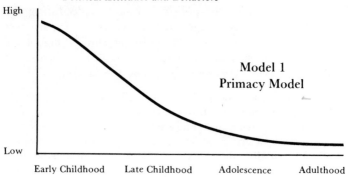

High

Model 1
Primacy Model

Low

Early Childhood   Late Childhood   Adolescence   Adulthood

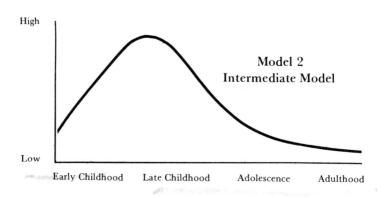

High

Model 2
Intermediate Model

Low

Early Childhood   Late Childhood   Adolescence   Adulthood

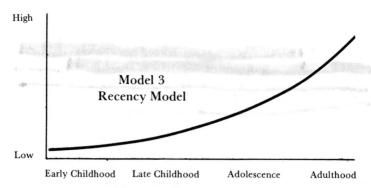

High

Model 3
Recency Model

Low

Early Childhood   Late Childhood   Adolescence   Adulthood

Source: Robert Weissberg, *Political Learning, Political Choice and Democratic Citizenship,* © 1974, p. 26. Reprinted by permission of Prentice-Hall, Inc., Englewood Cliffs, New Jersey.

PRIMACY MODEL

The *primacy model* asserts that early childhood is the period in which the most significant political socialization takes place. Important orientations concerning politics are acquired during early childhood. The individual tends to maintain these early acquired orientations as he or she grows older. These orientations tend to shape or structure the political choices made by the individual in later life. A statement by Easton and Dennis catches the essence of this argument and suggests the consequences of early learning for both the individual and the political system: [7]

> Those children who begin to develop positive feelings toward the political authorities will tend to grow into adults who will be less easily disenchanted with the system than those children who early acquire negative, hostile sentiments . . . basic childhood sentiments are less easily dislodged and modified than those acquired later in life.

In this interpretation of political socialization the early years are the crucial ones. Not very much significant political learning is presumed to take place during the adult years. The options for the adult in terms of what political beliefs and behaviors will be adopted are predetermined in large part by the basic preferences and attachments acquired during early childhood. The choices are structured by the earlier formed orientations. The fact that one develops attachments to free enterprise as a political and economic system during early childhood insulates one as an adult from the appeals of socialism. The establishment of a firm identification with one political party during childhood makes it difficult for the adult to support a candidate of another political party.

RECENCY MODEL

The *recency model* makes a different assertion about political learning. It holds that the closer a particular political learning experience is to relevant adult decisions and behavior, the greater its impact. The key to understanding adult political attitudes and behavior is to be found not so much in

[7] Easton and Dennis, *op. cit.*, pp. 106–107.

the distant experiences of childhood, but in more contemporaneous life. In this interpretation the adult's political perspectives are viewed as amenable to change. Adults tend to forget the information and ideas they were exposed to many years earlier. The imprint of the early years does not have the staying and structuring power presumed by the primacy model, and, thus, it is not so relevant to the political experiences of the adult years.

INTERMEDIATE-PERIOD MODEL

A third interpretation falls between the other two models. The *intermediate-period model* emphasizes the period between the early childhood years and adult experiences. As the middle graph in Figure V.1 illustrates, the emphasis in this model is upon late childhood and early adolescence. This model shares with the recency model the assumption that preadult experiences are important for adult political outlooks and behavior but it places greatest importance on a different time in the preadult years. The intermediate-period model fits in most closely with the cognitive-developmental theories of social and political learning discussed in Chapter IV. During late childhood and early adolescence the individual develops the capacity to understand political and social affairs.

In current discussions about political socialization each of these models has its adherents and its opponents. Like many disagreements in the social sciences the final differences may not be so much over the question of fact (what happens when) as over perceptions and evaluations — judgments as to what type of political learning can be considered the most significant. Each of these models seems particularly applicable for the understanding of different types of political learning.

The primacy model, with its emphasis upon early childhood and the persistence of early acquired orientations, is most useful for understanding basic political loyalties and identities. As suggested in Chapter IV, strong attachments to the political system and identifications with political symbols and authorities, along with other group identities, tend to be formed early and maintained throughout life. These basic orientations also tend to serve as filters or eyeglasses through which later political stimuli are perceived and classified by the individual. The taking on of the basic attachments, those identified in Chapter III as the basic or core aspect of the political self, seem to follow the basic outline of the primacy model. To the extent one holds that the formation of orientations such as these is the most significant aspect in the development of the political self, it is fair to claim that the primacy model is the best one for understanding political socialization.

The intermediate-period model seems to fit best the acquisition of information and understanding of political roles and processes — those orientations placed in the middle level in our discussion of aspects of the political self in Chapter III. During late childhood and early adolescence, the period emphasized in the intermediate-period model, the individual acquires the basic intellectual capabilities to understand the abstractions and relationships that make up the political world. (This aspect of political learning was discussed in the sections on late childhood and adolescence in Chapter IV.) If one holds this type of political learning to be the crucial component of the political self, the intermediate model may offer the best description of political learning.

The recency model, with its emphasis upon the adult years, is most applicable for explaining the day-to-day choices and decisions the adult makes with respect to political issues and events. Throughout life some aspects of the political world are constantly changing. New policies are formulated, new political leaders appear, and the processes for accomplishing political goals are altered. These changes often require the formation of new attitudes or changes in established ones. These types of political choices are the ones most likely to be influenced by political events and experiences in the adult years.

Each of these models, then, is useful for understanding a particular type of political learning. The relationship between the three models and types of orientations corresponds with the argument about the sequential development of political outlooks made in Chapter IV and with the three different aspects of the political self discussed in Chapter III. By tying together age periods and the types of political orientations we can suggest the developmental pattern graphed in Figure V.2. The more basic and broad political orientations tend to be acquired early in life. More specific political choices and decisions are concentrated through the adult period.

FIGURE V.2   *Scope of Political Orientation*

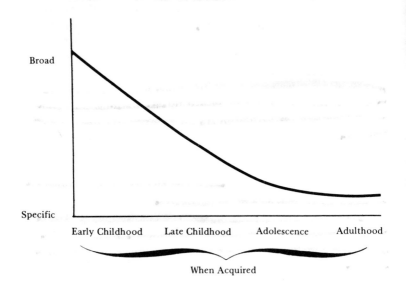

Source: Robert Weissberg, *Political Learning, Political Choice and Democratic Citizenship,* © 1974, p. 30. Reprinted by permission of Prentice-Hall, Inc., Englewood Cliffs, New Jersey.

By late adolescence the acquisition of the broad political attachments and the formation of general modes of political thinking have been accomplished. Adult political learning is characterized by more specific political decisions and the formation or alteration of more specific attitudes. For the most part early acquired outlooks are important for later life. Early acquired basic political outlooks are particularly resistant to change in the later years. On the other hand, other types of political orientations seem much more susceptible to change over the adult years. This is particularly so for specific issue beliefs and policy positions. The proposition that basic social and political identifications and general beliefs about political institutions tend to be more stable than beliefs about specific events, programs, and personalities has found support in at least one empirical investigation.[8] Continual acquisition or alteration of more specific beliefs and preferences is probably necessary if individuals are going to continue to relate to a political world that is never completely stable. Early socialization cannot prepare the individual for all that he or she must respond to or relate to in later life. In this sense childhood and adolescent political socialization cannot adequately complete the development of the political self.[9]

Political learning continues through adult life. Later political outlooks and behavior are constrained by early learning, but not completely determined. In some instances even the very basic political outlooks can be changed during the adult years. In the remainder of this chapter we consider two types of adult political socialization. First, we look at what might be called more "normal" additions or adjustments to the political self. Second, we discuss conditions that sometimes lead to changes in the more basic political outlooks during the adult years.

GENERAL ADULT POLITICAL LEARNING

For the most part political socialization during the adult years does not entail overall changes in basic political outlooks and identities. Dramatic across the board changes (such as the acquisition of basic political attachments and perspectives that take place in early childhood and the significant developments in political thinking that take place during late childhood and early adolescence) are not the rule during the

8 Donald Searing, Gerald Wright, and George Rabinowitz, "The Primacy Principle: Attitude Change and Political Socialization," *British Journal of Political Science*, 6 (1976), pp. 83–113.

9 For a discussion of incomplete socialization and why childhood socialization cannot adequately prepare the individual for adult life, see Arnold M. Rose, "Incomplete Socialization," *Sociology and Social Relations*, XLIV (1960), pp. 244–250.

adult years. Adult political learning normally entails things such as forming opinions on particular policies, becoming more or less involved with particular political events or activities, and forming reactions to various political leaders. The earlier acquired basic political identifications and perspectives tend to endure with only minor alterations.

A good portion of adult political learning results from stimuli from the political world. The rise of new issues calls for new or changed opinions on the part of the politically aware adult. Political leaders come and go. The citizen is called to make choices and evaluations of the new leaders. Political parties and other politically relevant groups may alter their programs or shift their alliances. Individuals who are tied to these groups must decide whether to go along with these changes. Particular political events may motivate the adult citizen to become more interested in politics and electoral activities. Other political events may lead to apathy or a sense of alienation. Choices like these constitute much of normal political learning during the adult years. In discarding old attitudes, forming new ones, or making alterations in long-lasting political perspectives the adult citizen is influenced by his close associates, by the groups to which he belongs, by the media to which he pays attention, and by the action and messages that come from the political world. It should be clear by this point how and why this type of political learning differs from that of the preadult years.

Universal age-related developments in political outlooks are not the fundamental substance of adult political socialization. However, there are some age patterns that are fairly common and deserve to be noted here. Movements from adolescence to young adulthood, from young adulthood to middle age, and from middle age to old age are not without consequences for political perspectives. These alterations are most often associated with changes in social roles, rather than innate developmental changes that are important in earlier years. Leaving the parental home, getting married, having children, going to college, taking a first job, changing jobs, and retiring from active work are all age-related changes that can alter or add to political orientations. The high school graduate who goes off to college may find himself exposed to political influences he or she did not have at home. The young men or women who leave home and begin to support themselves by working may look at tax policies and governmental services differently from when they lived in their parents' house. Having children and buying a house often lead one to become more concerned about schools and community affairs. The consequences of common adult experiences such as these are only beginning to receive much attention from students of socialization. More knowledge of how such changes in social roles affect political outlooks would certainly enrich our understanding of political socialization during the adult years.

The types of changes we are referring to are probably most apparent during the young adult period. The transition from adolescence to adulthood is a big step for most individuals. The assumption of adult roles is not completed overnight. For most individuals the late teens to the early thirties are years in which the young man or young woman slowly, tentatively, and hesitantly begins to take on various adult roles. This pattern holds for politics and citizen roles as it does in other areas. Many of the most visible political roles are not available to individuals until they become adults. This is true of electoral and participant roles, in particular.

Studies from the United States and other Western nations have found that the young adult years from the late teens into the early thirties constitute a period of growing interest and involvement in politics.[10] Over the twenties there is a steeper increase in voting turnout, in participation in campaign activities, in expressing an interest in politics, in having a sense of political involvement, and in identifying with a political party than in any other period of the adult years. This pattern is demonstrated by the data in Table V.1, which shows the proportion of a sample of adult Americans who report various types of political participation by age.

The changes over the young adult years can be explained best by relating them to the tendency of the young adult to

10 For a review of works suggesting this age pattern, see Lester W. Milbrath, *Political Participation: How and Why Do People Get Involved in Politics* (Chicago: Rand McNally, 1965), pp. 134–135.

TABLE V.1 *Increase in Political Involvement and Participation with Age: 1972*

				Age			
	18–19	20–24	25–29	30–39	40–49	50–59	60 and over
% who reported being "very interested" in following campaign [a]	17%	26%	30%	33%	33%	33%	34%
% reporting having written letter to public official [b]	11	24	27	31	34	24	22
% identifying as independents [c]	47	50	52	39	33	26	22
% reporting having voted for president in 1972 [d]	51	65	72	72	83	75	69

Source: Data taken from Survey Research Center 1972 National Election Study and made available through the Inter-University Consortium for Political Research.

[a] "Some people don't pay much attention to the political campaigns. How about you, would you say that you have been very much interested, somewhat interested, or not much interested in following the political campaigns so far this year?"

[b] "Have you ever written a letter to any public officials giving them your opinion about something that should be done?"

[c] "Generally speaking, do you usually think of yourself as a Republican, a Democrat, an Independent, or what?"

[d] "Who did you vote for in the election for president?"

become increasingly established in a particular social setting and to take on various adult social and economic roles. Political participation and involvement are closely tied to other forms of social participation and involvement. These are the years during which young adults generally leave the parental family and establish homes of their own. They get married and have children. They become established in a job or career or other adult position. Commenting on the growth in political party affiliation over this period among Norwegian voters, Henry Valen and Daniel Katz argue: [11]

> The critical point for strong identifications seems to be reached by age 30. The average Norwegian is more concerned with interests of a personal character as a young man and then becomes involved in political affairs as he takes on the roles of taxpayer, parent, and community member.

For most people the years between twenty and thirty represent an important time of exploration and provisional commitments to adult roles, memberships, relationships, and responsibilities. For many young adults it is still a period of growth and development in political awareness and thinking.

Alterations in political interest and perspectives probably accompany other changes in social roles for the adult citizen. Old age and retirement may result in consequences the opposite of those that occur in the young adult years. Retirement from active work may lead to a more general disengagement from social and political involvement as well as some important changes in dependency upon the government.

MORE BASIC CHANGES IN POLITICAL ORIENTATION DURING THE ADULT YEARS

In its more common form and substance adult political learning entails the formation and alteration of attitudes on more specific political issues and events. There are occasions, however, when even more basic political identities and perspectives can be altered during the adult years. Long-lasting identifications with a political party may be ruptured. Long-

---

[11] Henry Valen and Daniel Katz, *Political Parties in Norway* (Oslo: Universitets-Forlaget, 1964), pp. 211–212.

standing, fundamental orientations toward government can be
eroded or even wiped out. Adults sometimes move from one
end of the political spectrum to the other. We turn now to
outline some of the conditions that contribute to more fundamental changes in political outlooks among adults. We suggest
three different types of conditions: (1) societal-level events or
changes, (2) events or movements that affect particular groups,
and (3) individual changes in life situation.

SOCIETAL-LEVEL EVENTS OR CHANGES

For most basic political orientations the social and individual pressures are for persistence or stability. However, from
time to time general political or social events of significant
magnitude can cause large numbers of people to alter even
some of their most fundamental political outlooks. The American Civil War in the 1860s and the Great Depression of the
1930s were two such events in American history. These events
caused large numbers of Americans, many of them already
well into their adult years, to change basic perspectives on
their relationships with the national government, their expectations of what government should or should not do, and in
some instances their identification with a political party. The
achievement of national independence by African and Asian
states in the past thirty years, surrender for Germany and
Japan in 1945, political and social revolutions in the Soviet
Union, China, and Cuba are other examples of national or
societal events (some extremely traumatic) that have led to
significant, widespread alterations of important political outlooks among large numbers of people. The African tribesman
had to learn to identify with a new national government
where none had existed before. The German citizen, who had
been reared to believe in the inevitable expansion of German
power, had to learn to accept and live with a defeated Germany.

These examples all represent extremely traumatic national
events. Less dramatic occurrences or trends can also lead to
significant alterations in adult political outlooks. A good contemporary example of such a phenomena is the significant
drop in governmental trust among Americans over the past

decade. The sense that the government can be trusted and that political leaders are responsive to the interests of the people, or the opposite, would seem to be one of the basic general predispositions that tends to be acquired early and persists over time. Over the past decade, however, numerous Americans, older adults as well as younger, have experienced a significant erosion in the extent to which they feel government can be trusted and/or that it is responsive to the needs of the people. This trend has been discussed and documented in a number of different ways. The data presented in Table V.2 show very vividly the extent of this decline over the years from 1964 through 1974. In 1964, 22 percent of the sample of adult Americans responded that they thought the government in Washington could be trusted to do what is right *only* some or none of the time. Seventy-two percent of the respondents took that position in 1974. These trends suggest very significant changes in an important political orientation in the span of only a decade. The changes represented here cannot be

TABLE V.2   *Decrease in Governmental Trust and Responsiveness: 1964–74*

	1964	*1966*	*1968*	*1970*	*1972*	*1974*
% saying government can be trusted only some or none of time [a]	22%	32%	37%	45%	46%	63%
% saying governments works for benefit of few big interests rather than all of people [b]	30%	36%	41%	55%	57%	73%

Source: Data taken from Survey Research Center National Election Studies and made available through the Inter-University Consortium for Political Research.

[a] "How much of the time do you think that you can trust the government in Washington to do what is right — just about always, most of the time, only some of the time, or none of the time?"

[b] "Would you say the government is pretty much run by a few big interests looking out for themselves or that it is run for the benefit of all people?"

accounted for simply by the addition of new adults to the general population. The same substantial movement is apparent among older and middle-age citizens who entered the adult period before the dates of these surveys.

The trend of these data suggests two important points with respect to adult political socialization. First, the data suggest that among adults, significant alterations in even rather basic political perspectives are possible. Second, such general changes can occur as a result of political events and activities. The increase in negative feelings concerning the responsiveness and trustworthiness of American national government have resulted from a rapid cumulation of disillusionment among Americans. The Vietnam involvement, the efforts of the government to bring about racial integration, the credibility problems of the Johnson administration, and the set of activities popularly associated with Watergate lie behind this dramatic shift in political perspectives.

The tendency is for the more basic political orientations to persist through the adult years. However, they can be changed under the pressure of dramatic events and shifts in political, social, and economic conditions. Adult political outlooks continue to be influenced by what happens in the real world. When events are significant enough, they can dislodge or alter even those basic political orientations generally resistant to change.

EVENTS OF MOVEMENTS THAT AFFECT ONLY PARTICULAR GROUPS

We argued above that adult political orientations can be changed by large-scale societal events that tend to affect all segments of the population. Some events or movements may affect only particular segments of the population. They may alter the political perspectives of a particular subgroup, but have little impact on other people.

The Civil Rights movement, along with various manifestations toward black power or black consciousness, is probably the best example of such a group-relevant movement in recent United States history. The political consciousness of blacks and the sense that they should and can make demands on the system has been one consequence. Although the impact of the Civil Rights and black power movement has fallen disproportionately upon younger blacks, the political perspectives of many older blacks have also been influenced. Voting turnout among blacks has increased significantly since 1960, a period during which the voting turnout among most other segments of the population has tended to go down.

The youth movement of the late 1960s and the women's rights movement of the 1970s constitute other examples that have particular impacts on special populations. The youth movement with its stress on a "youth culture" and a "generation gap" played a role in altering or shaping the political outlooks of many young adults, especially those on college and university campuses. During the late 1960s and early 1970s the political outlooks of many young Americans were influenced in directions quite different from their earlier family and school political socialization. Early acquired feelings of trust for political authorities and respect for the system were undermined. Some young people were motivated to support and engage in various types of political protest activities. It is still too early to gauge whether the experiences and political expressions adopted by many young adults during this period will result in lasting influence on basic political orientations.

The women's rights movement, with its emphasis upon breaking down the traditional sex role categories, has led many women to adopt a more assertive role in social life and to become more actively involved in politics. For many women this has meant overcoming perceptions regarding political life that they acquired as a result of their own early political socialization. They have had to combat not only the positions of others but also many of their own deep seated impressions about the role of women. As was the case among blacks the impact of the women's rights movement has been greater among younger women. Many older women, however, have been influenced with respect to their own perspectives toward the position of women in political and social life.

CHANGES IN THE LIFE SITUATION OF INDIVIDUALS

More individualistic experiences also can lead to alterations in political outlooks. A significant change in one's so-

cial and economic positions can lead to alterations in even
more basic political orientations. We pointed out above that
the normal process of aging and taking on new societal roles
over the adult life period is often related to changes in political perspectives. Here we refer to a variation on that theme.
The focus here is on more substantial alterations in the position of the individuals, ones that often involve a substantial
break from earlier experiences. Changes such as these can lead
to basic transformations or discontinuities in political outlooks. A substantial change in economic position may lead to
a change in political party affiliation. Alterations in basic
political ideology may follow substantial changes in group
affiliations. Shifts in perspectives toward political authorities
can occur as a result of experiences the adult has with political participation and involvement.

An example may help make clear the types of changes we
have in mind: Tony was born into a working-class family. His
parents were second-generation Americans of Italian background. He lived in a neighborhood made up almost exclusively of other working-class families of Italian origins. He
was brought up in the Catholic church. Let us say that as a
young man he is bright and ambitious. He goes off to college,
and subsequently to law school. He is anxious "to make it," to
be regarded as successful according to the norms of the larger
society. He does well as a lawyer. He marries a girl from an
upper income Protestant family, and moves into a home in an
affluent, largely Protestant suburb. He gradually breaks most
of his childhood ties — with friends of earlier days, with the
"old neighborhood," with the Catholic church. He has only
limited association with members of his parental family.

In this example Tony makes a number of important breaks
with the setting of his early socialization. These breaks are
likely to be associated with changes in important political
perspectives. During childhood and youth the norms coming
from family, friends, and other associations pointed toward
identification with the Democratic party and support for political programs that would benefit the little man and the
working class. These messages were reinforced by the Italian-
American and Catholic identification. His new social environ-

ment confronts him with very different political influences. His law associates, his in-laws, his new neighbors, and many of the people he comes into contact with are likely to be Republicans and to support more conservative political positions. Given the substantial breaks he has made with his past and the mutual reinforcement he receives from his new environment he might be expected to substantially alter some of his early acquired basic political outlooks. He may switch to the Republican party, or become an independent. He may move in a conservative direction with respect to welfare state issues. He may become less concerned with the government working to help the little man and more concerned with preserving the existing order.

This may be a somewhat extreme example. It represents considerable discontinuity between the position of the childhood years and that of adulthood. However, it does suggest the types of changes that often lead to substantial alterations in political outlooks later in life. This example is presented to make two points. First, changes in social position do take place and they often lead to alterations even in some of the more basic political perspectives. Second, it generally takes rather substantial alterations in social and economic setting to alter sharply the basic loyalties and identities acquired during the early years. In many instances individuals can experience significant changes in life situations with little or no impact on early acquired basic political orientations. The political consequences of substantial changes in life situation can vary greatly from case to case.

Other types of significant changes in life during the adult years may also contribute to alterations in political perspectives. Movement from one part of the country to another, or from a rural area to a large city, may entail changes significant enough to cause discontinuities in basic political outlooks. Joining new groups or forming close ties with new people can also alter early acquired political orientations.

Unfortunately the impact of such changes upon political outlooks during the adult years has received little investigation. The Bennington College study conducted four decades ago is one of the few studies that carefully documents the

92 *Age and the Political Self: The Adult Years*

impact of a new life situation upon the political preferences of young adults. That study, conducted during the 1930s, found that over their years in college the Bennington College girls tended to move substantially to the left in their political outlooks. The movement away from affluent, conservative, Republican homes to the predominantly liberal college campus was followed by a leftward direction in political preferences.[12]

CONCLUSION

We have explored what happens to political outlooks during the adult years. For the most part adult political learning involves the adoption and alteration of more specific opinions and preferences. Much of it is influenced by events and personalities in the contemporary political world. For the most part adults maintain the basic political identifications and outlooks they acquired during the earlier years. These, more often than not, serve as foundation points or constraints governing later acquired, less basic political preferences. There are conditions that can even sharply alter these early acquired basic attachments. We have suggested several different types of conditions that can alter basic political orientations.

12 Theodore Mead Newcomb, *Personality and Social Change: Attitude Formation in a Student Community* (New York: Dryden Press, 1943).

CHAPTER VI

Methods of Political Learning

In chapters IV and V we explored the question of *when* in the life span political socialization takes place. We outlined the sequences of political learning and suggested what types of orientations tend to be acquired at what points. In this chapter we turn to the question of *how* political socialization is accomplished. Through what processes does the individual take on his or her particular political outlooks? Through what techniques do the agents of socialization pass on political information, values, and attitudes? The discussion of the preceding chapters should have made the reader aware that many different modes of political learning contribute to the formation of the political self and that different types of learning take place at different points in life. In this chapter we make distinctions between different modes of learning. We try to suggest how different techniques of learning contribute to the acquisition of different types of orientations.

Before considering the modes of political learning we remind the reader that political socialization involves an interaction between the individual and agents of socialization. Both the agent with its particular message and the individual with his or her particular needs and predispositions bring something to socializing experiences. Both affect the outcome of socialization.

There are two rather different emphases in conceptions of political socialization. One views political socialization primarily in terms of the transmission of political orientations from various agents of socialization to the individual being socialized. Parents pass on a political party preference and ideological positions to their offspring. Schools attempt to transmit both information and positive feelings about the nation to their students. At a societal level it is sometimes stated that political socialization involves the transmission of an existing political culture from one generation to the next. The other view focuses more on the development of the individual's own political consciousness and the formation of his or her particular manner of thinking about politics and political relationships. Different people have different ways of thinking about politics. There are great differences in the level of consciousness about politics among different people. The individual's needs and experiences, his or her capacity to reason and to understand, are seen as important ingredients in any political learning situation. This emphasis can be seen in the cognitive developmental interpretation of political learning. The young child perceives authority relationships in personal and idealized terms. He or she is not equipped mentally to handle more abstract and impersonal conceptions. The adolescent and adult are likely to be more sensitive to the complexities of political life. Their capacity to think and to understand has developed so the same stimuli from the political world or from agents of political socialization are received and understood very differently.

Although there are some general patterns in the development of political thinking — for example, most adults are capable of dealing with the abstractions of the political world better than most young children — the level of political consciousness and manner in which political stimuli are received remain individualized. Some people are very conscious or aware of what goes on in political life. Others seem to tune out political information and stimuli. A given political event or a given message from a socialization agent will be heeded and made meaningful in different ways by different individuals. The individualized components to political socialization should be kept in mind as we consider various modes of political learning in this chapter and as we move on to discuss agents of political socialization in the next few chapter.

TWO GENERAL FORMS OF POLITICAL SOCIALIZATION

Two very general formulations of political socialization have been identified in the literature on political socialization. These include (1) direct and (2) indirect forms of political learning. These two formulations constitute the first and basic distinction we make between different modes of political learning.

Indirect political socialization entails the initial acquisition of predispositions that are not in themselves political, but that influence the subsequent development of specifically political outlooks. Nonpolitical orientations are acquired first. They are later directed toward political objects to form political orientations. This form of political learning may be illustrated by a particular formulation of the way individuals acquire outlooks toward political authority. This formulation suggests that the child, as a result of his relationship with parents, siblings, teachers, and other close "nonpolitical" authorities, develops certain expectations regarding persons in positions of authority. From these personal experiences he develops a particular self-image regarding how he should relate to those in authority positions. In this manner the child acquires a general disposition toward authority; not only particular authorities, but authority in general. Later as he becomes aware of political authorities — for example, the policeman, the president, the mayor — this general predisposition towards authority is directed toward the more particular political authorities. On the basis of early experiences with his parents the young child comes to feel that authorities are kind and helpful. When he becomes aware of figures such as the policeman and the president he directs or generalizes the general predisposition acquired through relationships with parents onto the policeman and the president. They, too, are seen as kind and helpful.

Indirect political learning is a two-step process. First, a general predisposition is formed. At a later point that general predisposition is transferrred to particular political objects. The key to understanding just what form the specifically political orientation will take is in knowing something about the individual's general predispositions and which ones will be brought to bear on a particular political object. An individual learns not to trust other people; he or she comes to mistrust political leaders. An individual learns to assert himself to get what he wants; he or she becomes an assertive citizen.

Direct political socialization refers to processes in which the content of orientations transmitted is specifically political. Whereas indirect political socialization entails a two-step process, the direct form involves the initial transmission of explicitly political outlooks. The individual learns explicitly about the structure of his or her government, the virtue of a particular party, or the superiority of his or her nation over all others. No intermediary general predisposition is involved in direct political socialization.

The notions of indirect and direct learning should not be confused with distinctions between intentional and unintentional socialization. It is tempting to pair indirect with unintentional and direct with intentional political socialization. Such pairing is misleading. It impairs the utility of both distinctions. Direct political socialization may be intentional and overt, as when the school teacher urges his or her pupils to be good citizens and to abide by the laws. Or direct learning may be unintentional as when the child picks up a fear of the police as a result of overhearing older siblings recount how they were beaten by a policeman. Indirect socialization may be intentional, as when the child is told that a "good boy" is one who obeys what he is told by adults; or unintentional, as when the child learns the necessity of rules by participating in neighborhood sports. The critical distinction between indirect and direct modes of learning is not the overt intent of the socialization agent, but whether or not the initial socialization experience is infused with specific political content.

Both modes of learning are common in the overall process of political socialization. Both have received attention from students of political learning. Early conceptions of political socialization tended to emphasize indirect political learning. More recent analysis has maybe overemphasized the direct modes of learning. The development of the political self, however, does not entail the prevalence of one form to the exclusion of the other. Some types of political orientations are more likely to be acquired through direct political learning and others through indirect forms of socialization. For example, identification with a particular political party is most often transmitted directly to an individual by his family, his close associates, or groups to which he belongs. Political predispositions such as political trust, political competence, and political assertiveness may result from indirect forms of political learning. More general self-concepts may be acquired first and only later transferred to political objects.

INDIRECT FORMS OF POLITICAL SOCIALIZATION

Some of the early discussions of political socialization stressed the indirect mode of learning. The transference of predispositions in nonpolitical situations to political objects was stressed. This emphasis stemmed largely from the influence of culture-personality and psychocultural-anthropology studies from which early conceptions of political socialization were borrowed.[1]

The psychocultural theories attempted to explain culture by analyzing the configuration of its personality types. In explaining the development of these personality traits they focused on the cultural context and the socialization experiences that gave rise to them. The major emphasis was on the experiences of the very young child within the famly context. Close fits were often discovered between the child-rearing practices used in a society and the personality traits or cultural patterns of adults.[2] The basic structure of individual personality was presumed to be formed during the first few years. Subsequent individual development is determined by these early dispositions. Explicit political orientations, as well as other types of specific social attitudes and values, are viewed as projections or generalizations from the basic personality

[1] For an examination of this influence on the notion of political socialization, see Gabriel Almond and Sidney Verba, *The Civic Culture* (Princeton: Princeton University Press, 1963), pp. 323–330.

[2] See John W. M. Whiting and Irwin L. Child, *Child Training and Personality* (New Haven: Yale University Press, 1953).

traits acquired early in life. The early development of personality attributes, such as self-esteem, ego-strength, authoritarianism, need for power, self-competence, are seen as related to the acquisition of political attitudes in later life.

Many of these notions were brought into the study of political learning as scholars attempted to explain the development both of individual political orientations and the collective political culture. A good example of how these ideas influenced early discussions of political socialization is suggested in the work of Gabriel Almond. Pointing out the differences between indirect and direct political learning, he suggested that the most important political socialization occurs through indirect processes. He stressed the important role of early family experiences in shaping general personality traits and interpreted political orientations as projections from these traits.[3] In a further elaboration of the psychocultural emphasis in political socialization analysis, Almond and Sidney Verba wrote:

> The early psychocultural approach to the subject regarded political socialization as a rather simple process. Three assumptions were usually made: (1) the significant socialization experiences that will affect later political behavior take place quite early in life; (2) these experiences are not manifestly political experiences, but they have latent political consequences — that is, they are neither intended to have political effects nor are these effects recognized, and (3) the direction of socialization is a unidirectional one: the more "basic" family experiences have a significant impact upon the secondary structures but are not in turn affected by them.[4]

Although Almond and Verba argued that the psychocultural approach unduly simplifies political socialization and does not explain the range of political characteristics that go into making the political self, the emphasis upon early childhood learning and upon the significance of basic general personality and social values to affect political orientations continues to be important. The importance of early childhood

[3] Gabriel A. Almond, "A Functional Approach to Comparative Politics," in Gabriel Almond and James S. Coleman (eds.), *The Politics of the Developing Areas* (Princeton: Princeton University Press, 1960), p. 28.
[4] Almond and Verba, *op. cit.*, p. 323.

learning and its consequences for adult political life was stressed in Chapters IV and V. Here we look more systematically at some of the more specific interpretations through which this indirect mode of political socialization is accomplished. We discuss: (1) interpersonal transference, (2) apprenticeship, and (3) generalization formulations of indirect political learning.

INTERPERSONAL TRANSFERENCE

One type of indirect political learning has been identified by Robert Hess and Judith Torney as *interpersonal transference.* They outline the assumptions of this form of learning as follows:

> This model assumes that the child approaches explicit political socialization already possessing a fund of experience in interpersonal relationships and gratifications. By virtue of his experience as a child in the family and as a pupil in the school, he has developed multifaceted relationships with figures of authority. In subsequent relationships with figures of authority, he will establish modes of interaction which are similar to those he has experienced with persons in his early life.[5]

Of the three forms of indirect political socialization we discuss, interpersonal transference is the closest to the psychocultural heritage discussed above. The interpersonal transference method has been applied primarily to explain the development of orientations toward authority. The question of how the child will perceive political authorities is presumed to be rooted in his earliest contact with more immediate nonpolitical authorities, especially his parents. As the child becomes aware of the political world and authority figures in it, he transfers the feelings he has developed with respect to earlier and more personal authorities onto the more distant political figures. David Easton and Robert Hess explain this mechanism in this way:

> The authority figures with which they (children) have earliest and most intimate contact are of course their parents, and it is this image of authority that they subsequently seem to trans-

[5] Robert D. Hess and Judith V. Torney, *The Development of Political Attitudes* (Chicago: Aldine, 1967), p. 20.

fer to political figures that cross their vision. The child not only learns to respect and admire political authorities, but with regard to many characteristics sees them as parents writ large.[6]

In his early study of the development of authority orientations among American school children, Fred Greenstein also allows that the favorable orientations toward the president as a central authority figure may result from the transference of feelings toward the parents to the political world.[7]

This interpretation of political learning has been offered to explain the early acquisition of the highly benevolent feelings toward political authorities that seem to be universal among young children. Its applicability to the learning of other types of political outlooks would seem to be limited. As we pointed out in Chapter IV this interpretation is only one of several that have been offered to explain the benevolent image given political authorities by young children.

APPRENTICESHIP

A second mode of indirect learning, apprenticeship, is closely related to the interpersonal transference model. *Apprenticeship,* as in the case of interpersonal transference, entails transferring developmental experiences from the nonpolitical to the political world. Although the interpersonal transference form entails the direct transference of explicit predispositions acquired through experiences with nonpolitical role models, apprenticeship learning occurs as the individual acquires skills and values used in a specifically political context. Nonpolitical activities are viewed as practice or apprenticeship for political activities. From various nonpolitical experiences the individual acquires skills and insights he uses to find his way in the political world.

In the United States, character-training organizations such as the Scouts, 4-H clubs, and Little Leagues are important for this form of political learning. In such organizations a child

[6] David Easton and Robert D. Hess, "The Child's Political World," *Midwest Journal of Political Science,* VI (1962), p. 242.

[7] Fred I. Greenstein, "The Benevolent Leader: Children's Images of Political Authority," *American Political Science Review,* LIV (1960), p. 941.

learns to compete, but to compete only within the rules; he learns to want to win, but to accept defeat with grace; he learns to choose leaders by popular vote, and to punish their mistakes by voting them out of office. He learns, among other things, how to act in competitive but regulated situations. One of the present concerns about Little League, hockey teams, and other competitive sports is that this positive socialization in democratic behavior is being tempered by parental enthusiasm for "winning at all costs." This emphasis on "winning" both changes the interactions involved in "playing the game," with increased anxiety and concern over losing, and changes the criteria for success. Instead of learning the fun of competition and acceptance of defeat, many Little Leaguers are disgraced if they fail to win the game. Without belaboring the point, the overstress on "winning at all costs" as a positive value also can be seen transferred to the political arena in what has become known as the "Watergate mentality."

The idea of apprenticeship learning also has been applied to the analysis of participation and authority. Almond and Verba, suggesting modifications in psychocultural hypotheses, include school and work experiences as nonpolitical settings in which apprenticeship learning take place. They retain the ideas of indirect political learning and the analogy from nonpolitical to political situations. Using the school and work setting in addition to the family, the age of indirect learnng experiences is expanded to include late childhood and adolescence (school) and adulthood (work). Expanding the notion of indirect political socialization to include training for political roles or what we have identified as apprenticeship, they point out that:

> . . . the role that an individual plays within the family, the school, or the job may be considered training for the performance of political roles. . . . Participation in non-political decision making may give one the skills needed to engage in political participation: the skills of self-expression and a sense of effective political tactics.[8]

---

8 Almond and Verba, *op. cit.,* pp. 327–328.

Two important aspects of indirect political socialization hypotheses are suggested here. First, indirect political socialization is not arrested in childhood but continues throughout life. Second, indirect political learning is not restricted to transference of expectations from nonpolitical role models to political persons. It includes also the acquisition of skills, habits, behaviors, and practices appropriate for political activities.

The data collected by Almond and Verba in the five-nation study support these contentions. Participatory experiences in the family, school, and job are all related to the quality of participation in political life. Almond and Verba also find that the effect of participation in the making of decisions in these three settings is cumulative. The individual who has consistent opportunities for participation in each of the three nonpolitical areas is more likely to generalize the effect of such participation to the political world than the individual who participated in one nonpolitical area but not in others.[9] Family experiences, although important, are neither the only nor necessarily the most significant exposures that help prepare individuals for participation in the political world. Union participation may actively further democratic values and give workers participatory experiences for political life.[10] Participating in nonpolitical decision making in later life may offset the lack of such opportunities in childhood. Active participatory experiences in several areas would tend to reinforce positive feelings of self-competence and efficacy for the individual.

The stress on apprenticeship experiences is a major underpinning of the women's rights movement today. Women, to a much less extent than men, are afforded the participatory opportunities discussed above. From early childhood experiences on, girls are given much less opportunity than boys to acquire the skills and abilities to enable them to compete successfully in the political world. Girls' toys tend to be more passive than the more stimulating mechanical toys given to boys. Boys are encouraged to be adventurers, builders, creators, leaders. Girls,

[9] *Ibid.*, p. 366.
[10] Seymour Martin Lipset, Martin A. Trow, and James S. Coleman, *Union Democracy* (Glencoe, Ill.: The Free Press, 1956).

to a great extent, are still presented with role models and cues to be attractive, popular, and passive. Growing up, boys are encouraged in team sports and active physical play, but girls are still for the most part ostracized from these activities. Although Little Leagues are opening their doors to girls, and universities are being pressured to supply adequate support for women's athletics, the biases against active assertive women are still built into the American culture. The feeling of "second-class" citizenship that many women perceive has always been one of the dominant arguments for women's colleges. The argument, which would be much the same for black-controlled schools, is that at an all-women's college the leadership opportunities, scholastic competition, and dominant values would favor participation of women, and hence apprenticeship learning. This opportunity to be in the dominant group has been also favored by many black leaders urging "community control" of their schools.

The transfer relationship may proceed in both directions. Democratic norms and opportunities for participation in the political world may generate pressure for democratic arrangements and the right to participate in nonpolitical situations, as well as the other way around. Thus, as women become more active in leadership positions in the political world, there will be more of an outcry for changes in the nonpolitical world. As black people have achieved more political opportunities, they have put more stress upon membership participation and democratic forms in secondary organizations, schools, and even work groups. Contemporary American college students have successfully pressured for increased student participation in the making of university policies by taking democratic values and rights from the political world and arguing that they should be followed within the university. They have argued that since we live in a democracy and presume to follow democratic procedures as a nation, university decisions should also be made according to democratic procedures. This became a major aspect of the rationale of students demanding more "student power." In developing nations, demands for popular participation in political life are followed by demands for popular participation in labor unions, schools, and even the family. If it can be assumed that the sharing of decision-making authority in the family can help maintain the democratic state, it is also likely that the democratic state helps to activate participatory demands elsewhere in the society.

GENERALIZATION

A variation of indirect political socialization — generalization — is closely related to the two major forms already reviewed. In many instances social values are extended toward specifically political objects. A person's political self is embedded in his entire belief system. Verba writes persuasively on this point:

> The basic belief and value patterns of a culture — those general values that have no reference to specific political objects — usually play a major role in the structuring of political culture. Such basic belief dimensions as the view of man's relation to nature, as time perspective, as the view of human nature and of the proper way to orient toward one's fellow man, as well as orientations toward activity and activism in general would be clearly interdependent with specifically political attitudes.[11]

The notion of the political self being embedded in a total belief system is important in considering the various subcultures even within the United States. These cultures are often developed around social and economic, ethnic, or racial groupings. V. O. Key has written that southern politics has its own style based on regional distinctions.[12] The fact that inner-city black children have less political trust for political leaders or lower political efficacy may be part of the generalization from their social values to political objects.[13] The process, then, by which various subgroups in our society acquire

[11] Sidney Verba, "Comparative Political Culture," in Lucian W. Pye and Sidney Verba (eds.), *Political Culture and Political Development* (Princeton: Princeton University Press, 1965), pp. 521–522.

[12] V. O. Key, Jr., *Southern Politics in State and Nation* (New York: Knopf, 1949).

[13] See Edward S. Greenberg, "Orientations of Black and White Children to Political Authority Figures," *Social Science Quarterly*, 51 (1970), pp. 561–571.

their belief system contains latent consequences for political learning.

SUMMARY

The discussion of indirect political socialization suggests several conclusions. First, the initial emphasis of the psychocultural approach on child-rearing practices is unduly restrictive. Such an approach either fails to explain adequately, or does not allow for, important political socialization that takes place later in life. Rigid adherence to the psychocultural hypothesis would require that one interpret all postchildhood socialization as projections or extrapolations from the basic personality traits developed in early childhood. Second, indirect socialization encompasses types of learning other than the transference from role-models, which has been its major focus. We have suggested that part of the transference may be based on maturation development rather than on specific models, along with two additional forms of learning: apprenticeship and generalization. Third, empirical work using indirect political socialization models has focused on a narrow range of political orientations: those directed toward authority relationships and participation. Of course, it may be that these are the political orientations for which indirect learning is most significant. Indirect political socialization is unlikely to be as important for, say, acquiring a sense of national patriotism, party identification, or issue positions. To explain other aspects of political learning, it is necessary to consider also *direct* forms of political socialization.

DIRECT FORMS OF POLITICAL SOCIALIZATION

The second general category under which we can distinguish modes of political socialization is the notion of *direct* learning. Here we refer to experiences in which learning is explicitly political in nature. Just as we discussed several variations of indirect political socialization, we can suggest several forms of direct political learning: (1) imitation, (2) anticipatory political socialization, (3) political education, and (4) political experiences.

IMITATION

Imitation is the most extensive and persistent mode of social learning known to man.[14] Young and old, the intelligent and those less so, depend on imitative learning. Imitative learning is applicable to a wide array of values, behaviors, skills, expectations, and attitudes. The importance of imitation in social learning is obvious by watching a child learn to walk and talk. The most basic skills the individual acquires, mobility and communication, are acquired by the child in large part by imitating what he or she sees and hears.[15]

Imitative learning may be a conscious, deliberate effort, or it may involve unconscious copying of values and behavioral patterns from others. Consciously or not, children pick up an important part of social, cultural, and religious preferences from adults by taking parental values and adopting them as their own.

More than half of the children studied by Greenstein and by Easton and Hess had formed some sort of identification with a political party by age seven or eight. Since it is doubtful that many of the parents or teachers specifically taught political party identification to the children at this early age, it is likely that the children came to express a party preference by copying their parents. In later years teachers, friends, spouses, and work associates, as well as more public persons and opinion leaders, become sources of political values and attitudes, also by imitation. The close correspondence in political outlooks found among peers and work associates seems to indicate that imitation of some sort serves as a means of socialization within such relationships.

Although social imitation has been at the heart of theories of socialization and attitude acquisition, such as small-group analysis, reference-group theory, symbolic-interaction theory,

[14] For a discussion of the role of imitation in social learning, see Neal M. Miller and John Dollard, *Social Learning and Imitation* (New Haven: Yale University Press, 1941).

[15] See, for example, Frederick Elkin, *The Child and Society* (New York: Random House, 1960), ch. 3; and Albert Bandura, "Social-Learning Theory of Identificatory Processes," in David A. Goslin (eds.), *Handbook of Socialization Theory Research* (Chicago: Rand McNally, 1969), ch. 3.

and the social-adjustment function,[16] proximity seems to be only one aspect in this mode of political socialization. Certainly children imitate the party identification of their parents because they are significant persons in their lives. The proximal politics hypothesis, though, is insufficient for explaining the ideological development among all the politically active. Under the argument of proximity, we might expect the children of politically active people to become both politically active and ideological themselves, but this is not necessarily the case. Richard Merelman argues that although some people were surrounded by the politics of their parents at early ages, with both political influence and a set of ready-made contacts proximate to them, they often resist "the call to political action." Others from backgrounds of political apathy, removed from the proximity of political influences, enter into political careers or take on active roles in political life.[17] This argument stresses that proximity does *not* account for the varying patterns of political ideology, interest, and activity that seems to be present in the population. Although Merelman puts the stress on successful child-rearing practices, with the family having the prominent role in setting the example, imitation here reflects the complexities of family relationships. Various factors, discussed more extensively in Chapter VII, are important in the family transmission process. Certainly the parents' presentation of a consistent and congruent picture of their political ideology, interest, and activity affects the child's ability to imitate his or her parents. The importance of political life for the parents and the closeness of the parent-child relationship also will be important.

The obverse of political imitation is a situation in which the child deliberately rejects the values of parents or other authorities. This is a sort of negative imitation, or what reference-group theorists call a *negative reference-group effect*.[18] It is an

16 M. Brewster Smith, Jerome S. Bruner, and Robert W. White, *Opinions and Personality* (New York: Wiley, 1956), pp. 39–47.

17 Richard M. Merelman, "The Development of Political Ideology: A Framework for the Analysis of Political Socialization," *American Political Science Review*, 63 (1969), pp. 750–767.

18 See Herbert H. Hyman, "Reflections on Reference Groups," *Public Opinion Quarterly*, XXIV (1960), pp. 383–396.

act of rebellion. Reverse imitation sometimes takes place among adolescents, as they seek to shape an identity that differentiates them from parents and other authorities. Under certain conditions (when politics is highly salient to both the rebel and the ones rebelled against), this process can significantly alter the political self. The classic example of such rebellion is the youth from a conservative upper or middle-class home who joins a radical political group as an act of rebellion against his parents. The basic dynamics of rejecting the values of the imitated are similar to those taking place when the values are adopted.

ANTICIPATORY SOCIALIZATION

The *anticipatory socialization* mode of learning, similar to imitation is appropriately labeled by sociologist Robert Merton.[19] People who hope for professional jobs or high social positions frequently begin to take on the values and behavior associated with those roles long before they actually occupy them. This is most clearly seen in professional schools. Law students and medical students, for instance, begin to think and act like lawyers and doctors. This has also been the typical situation in boy and girl role playing, with the girl "mothering" the doll, while the boy plays the "boss." As some of these sex stereotype roles have begun to change, or at least more choices in roles offered, expected anticipatory behavior becomes less well-defined.

This type of socialization is less obvious in the analysis of political learning, but it undobtedly occurs. Student activists often begin to prepare themselves for elective office before they are old enough to vote. In anticipation of holding a position of political power in the future, they begin to take on mannerisms and styles they considered appropriate for the politician. The role of "good citizen" may be so well-defined by parents and teachers that the child can anticipate and prepare himself or herself for it. If good citizens are supposed to be knowledge-

[19] Robert K. Merton, *Social Theory and Social Structure* (New York: The Free Press, 1949), p. 265.

able about public affairs, the child may begin to read the newspaper or to choose the weekly news readers at school.

POLITICAL EDUCATION

The term *political education* is applied to direct, deliberate attempts to transmit political orientations. Instruction in politics is carried on by the family, the schools, political or governmental agencies, and innumerable groups and organizations. Unlike imitation and anticipatory socialization, the initiative in this form of political socialization is taken by the socializer rather than the individual being socialized. The school system consciously stresses informed participation as the basis of good citizenship, orders weekly news readers for the students, and puts aside time in class for the students to read the papers and discuss public affairs, rewarding them with grades for their active participation.

Most societies have both formal and informal channels for the direct teaching of socially valued political attitudes and behavior. As discussed in Chapter II, system maintenance is a high priority of any political system. The importance of political education is apparent. In the first place, citizens need some minimal information about political duties and rights to operate in the political arena. Obeying laws, especially those concerned with paying taxes, protection of property, and concern for the rights of others, is critical if governments are to operate effectively. Citizens ignorant of their obligations will serve neither themselves nor the state. We thus expect that, at a minimum, a society will establish some means of educating new citizens in their political duties and responsibilities. Along with this minimal political education, most societies make available to their citizens extensive information about their government and how it works. Perhaps even more importantly, the society will encourage and provide methods of political education to teach loyalty, patriotism, and support for the political institutions. Most formal schooling includes in the curriculum a full ritual life — pledging allegiance, saluting the flag, commemorating national heroes, celebrating national holidays, and so on — which is intended to bind the child affectively to the nation.

POLITICAL EXPERIENCES

A final type of direct political socialization results from political experiences. Although the notion of political experiences to some extent overlaps the concept of political education, the emphasis here is more on the person being socialized rather than the socializer. The children who have dressed up in Indian costumes and pilgrim hats to dance around to music, in anticipation of sharing in a Thanksgiving feast, are being politically educated — through a participatory experience. Many important political socialization experiences take place in such prepolitical and extrapolitical settings. The question of to what extent the desired values and goals of the socializer (in this case the classroom teacher) have succeeded may depend to a great extent on the success of the experience for the individuals involved. This emphasis on individual perception is to suggest once more the notion of the individual as an active participant in the socialization process.

Political experience is not randomly or evenly distributed within society. Some people participate more than others. Some people choose to be more actively and directly involved in politics. The student who runs for class office, the person who manages a friend's political campaign, the activist who makes a run for political office, have all demonstrated direct interest and involvement in the political process.

The classic formulation of the importance of political participation is found in the work of de Tocqueville.[20] The concept that much of what a person comes to believe and know about politics follows from his observations of and experiences in the political process has become part of our political culture. Traveling through early nineteenth-century America and watching the young republic struggle with the issues of democracy, liberty, and equality, de Tocqueville observed that participation in making political decisions in itself pro-

---

[20] Alexis de Tocqueville, *Democracy in America*, Vol. I (New York: Knopf, 1960), p. 322.

duces a sense of political responsibility. When a person feels he can participate in directing his social and political destiny he is more likely to adopt a pragmatic approach to politics. He learns to compromise, to accept when he must even policies that are counter to his own wishes. This assumption concerning the positive values of participatory experiences found in the writings of de Tocqueville have continued to be reflected in the political process. Such policies as the passage of the 1964 Economic Opportunity Act, with its statutory requirement of "maximum feasible participation" of the people affected by the programs, was based on the contention that observation of and involvement in the political process can substantially shape political orientations.

How and whether people do participate or not, however, is as much a function of the distribution of resources needed to participate as it is a reflection of the formal structure of the polity itself and the norm of the appropriateness of participation in that political culture. Participation costs are particularly high for the less well-educated, the unskilled, rural dwellers, ethnic minorities, and poor people. These groups tend to have less of the social resources of leisure time, money, and access to information than other groups in our society. Psychological resources also discriminate among people who tend to participate more in the political system. Those individuals who feel they can influence events, believe in the responsibility of citizenship, understand politics, and are not preoccupied with personal problems, who have considerable self-confidence, and are trusting of others, would tend to find it easier to participate. Finally, political activity for most people is not sustained beyond the achievement or disposal of the issues or problems that originally activated their participation. Thus, the suburbanite threatened by a potential zoning change, the parent concerned over the "bussing" of his child, teachers agitated over threats to the tenure system, all tend to resume their nonparticipatory status once their interests have been protected or the issue resolved.

Political experiences provide an important learning tool for political socialization. The consequences of the political experiences, though, may not be positive for either the individual or the political system: the suburbanite may lose his fight to keep the zoning change from being approved; the parent may feel ineffectual in the determination of his child's education; the teachers may continue to feel threatened over the possibility of losing their jobs. Political experiences may cause the participants to feel frustration, hostility, and alienation toward the political process and the people involved in making the authoritarian decisions. Thus, involvement may or may not have positive personal benefits for the participant and may or may not have beneficial consequences for broader societal concerns. As pointed out in Chapter II, however, generalized support for the political system seems to be based on more than simply "winning" on a particular issue.

From the perspective of the political system, certain political experiences are considered to be inappropriate. Whether the stress is on the system or the hegemony models discussed in Chapter II, political authorities oppose some kinds of political activities. Political experiences involved in burning draft cards, violent confrontations in the streets, and even more accepted civil disobedience of the sort espoused by Martin Luther King and Caesar Chavez, generate considerable opposition within the American society. Thus, although political experiences provide an important method by which people learn, these experiences are not always approved nor are they equally distributed in any political system. People with greater political influence are more able to derive benefits from political participation.

SUMMARY

We have reviewed three types of indirect and four types of direct modes of political learning. This review should suggest the complexity and variety of processes through which individuals acquire their political orientations. These modes of political learning are not mutually exclusive. In the overall process of political socialization each of these techniques for acquiring political orientations is likely to play a part. A variety of learning techniques may even contribute to the acquisition of a particular type of political outlook. We have tried to suggest what types of learning are most closely related to particular stages in political maturation and to particular types of political outlook. The benevolent orientations toward authorities among young children, which we discussed in Chapters II and IV, may be influenced by interpersonal transference, political education or indoctrination, and imitation — all at the same time.

Direct political socialization is probably most applicable to the acquisition of political information and knowledge and for the formation of political identifications. It is also the most common technique through which adults acquire their attitudes toward specific political issues. Indirect political socialization seems more relevant to the development of the more general ways in which the individual relates himself to the political world. One's general predispositions toward authorities, his tendency to trust or not trust political leaders, his feeling of competence to understand and influence the political world may often, though not always, involve the relating of general personal needs and predispositions to the political world.

It is difficult to examine systematically the mechanisms through which persons acquire their political views. It is easier to identify the views that citizens have and to discover what agencies influence these viewpoints than to analyze the particular learning processes intervening between the socialization agents and the values or attitudes acquired.

CHAPTER VII

The Family and Political Socialization

THE FAMILY AS A SOCIALIZING AGENT

The family universally serves as one of the most important sources of socialization.[1] Whether one poses the question from the standpoint of what agencies are important in transmitting basic social attachments, information, and values to new generations; or from the standpoint of how individuals develop their particular self-concepts, the family is identified as a significant influence. The relative significance of the family in overall socialization may vary, but the family impact looms large both in more traditional societies and in more highly developed and complex societies.

Two conditions contribute to the primary role of the family in socialization. First, the family has considerable access to individuals being socialized. During the early formative years this access often approaches a monopoly. Most theories of personality formation, child development, and socialization hold that the early years are very significant in the formation of basic personality and social and personal identities. If the ideas to which the child is exposed and the interpersonal relationships developed during the first few years of life are important, the family, because of its unique access, must play a primary role. Parents pass on ideas and information about the world — what is acceptable and unacceptable behavior, how individuals should relate to others, and so on. Parents and

[1] See, for example, Frederick Elkin, *The Child and Society: The Process of Socialization* (New York: Random House, 1960).

114

older siblings serve as important role models for the maturing child. The significant interpersonal relationships the individual has during the first few years are usually within the family.

The second basis of this significant influence is the strength of the ties formed among members of the same family. The socializing impact of associations depends, in part, upon the intensity of emotional and personal ties. The stronger the attachment, the more personal the ties, the more influence a given association will have. This, of course, is why primary relationships are so influential. Few human relationships match the strength of that established between parent and child, and in some instances among siblings in the same family.

The combined impact of extensive access and strong personalized ties puts the family in a position to have a significant impact on socialization. Most discussions of the role of the family in social learning focus on the impact of parents upon their young offspring. The family can continue to influence social and political outlooks throughout one's life. Communication and strong emotional ties among family members do not cease after childhood and youth.

THE FAMILY AND POLITICAL SOCIALIZATION

The role of the family in general socialization has been investigated extensively.[2] A variety of different theories have been developed to explain how and why this influence takes place. To some extent it is fair to say that the role of the family in the formation of the political self parallels its role in general socialization. Political learning is one particular form of social learning and follows similar patterns. We caution against carrying this analogy too far. There are reasons why one should expect the family to play a less prominent role in specifically political socialization.

First, many explicitly political roles and relationships are reserved for adult life. Much of adult political involvement

[2] For most of this chapter, when we consider the family as an agent of socialization, we are referring to the relationship between parents and their offspring, especially during childhood and adolescence. At the end of this chapter we discuss other family structures that affect political learning.

entails relating to contemporary political issues, governmental arrangements and leaders, and political groups. The period in life when the individual is most politically conscious and involved is far removed from childhood when the impact of the family looms so large. Other influences can intervene between the early influence of the family and the political context of adult life. The structure of political life also may differ from what existed during childhood.

Second, families generally do not take as much care in preparing their offspring for political life as they do for some other roles. Politics is not a high priority concern for most families. Nor is the political world particularly salient for most children and youths. Preparing their offspring for occupational and family roles ranks higher among the concerns of most parents than preparation for political life. Parents may be concerned explicitly with preparing their children to become self-supporting adults. Daughters, in particular, but also sons, may be socialized with respect to household roles so they will be ready for marriage and parenthood. Many families make an effort to see that their children receive appropriate religious training. In most families, however, little explicit thought or effort is directed toward political and civic training.

We do not mean to suggest that the family is not significant in political socialization, but merely to warn against relying too heavily on the assumption of commonality between political socialization and other socialization. The family influences political learning in three distinct ways. A brief description of each of these will aid in understanding the family role.

PASSING ON EXPLICITLY POLITICAL ORIENTATIONS

Through prescription, through discussion, by expressing their own outlooks, and through the example of their own political involvement (or lack of involvement), parents pass on political attitudes and evaluations to their children. Attitudes of the older generation concerning governmental trust and responsiveness might be conveyed to children through casual conversation. Parents may suggest, or even demand, that their children support one political party or another. Parents may warn their offspring of the dangers of some governmental actions and the values of others. By being active in political and community affairs and articulating their importance, parents contribute to the development of positive feelings regarding civic and political participation among their children.

Using the terminology of Chapter VI, we say the family carries out various forms of "direct" political socialization. The explicitness with which this is done varies, as does the content of what is conveyed. Because parents are in a position to influence their children so greatly during the early years, the political lessons acquired through the family can be significant.

INFLUENCE ON POLITICALLY RELEVANT ORIENTATIONS

The passing on of explicitly political lessons is only one way the family affects political socialization. As we pointed out above, the family plays an important part in shaping the basic personality, the social outlooks, and the self-concept of the maturing child. To the extent that these factors condition how individuals relate to the political world, the family can be said to influence political learning in this indirect way. On the bases of interpersonal relationships within the family and the teaching of parents and siblings, the individual learns to relate to others. He develops a sense of his own worth. He learns to trust people or not to trust them. He feels a sense of competence in making decisions or expects others to make them for him. These personal outlooks often are transferred onto the political world. A sense of interpersonal trust may be generalized to a sense of political trust. Feelings of self-competence may lead to political competence. In these respects the family leaves its imprint through "indirect" political socialization.

DETERMINING EXPOSURE TO OTHER SOCIALIZATION INFLUENCES

The family influences or conditions political socialization in yet another way. It plays an important role in determining what other agents of socialization the individual will be exposed to and what groups will serve as important political reference points. The friends one has, the schools one attends, and the religious and recreational groups one participates in during childhood and youth are determined in large part by the geographic and social position provided by the family. The offspring of a white family in an affluent suburb is likely to be exposed to a different set of socializing associations and influences than the black whose family lives in the inner-city ghetto. In this way the family has lasting impact on its offspring.

THE IMPACT OF THE FAMILY UPON POLITICAL LEARNING

We have discussed why the family is in a position to influence political learning and have suggested several means through which that impact is carried out. The question of how much of a role the family actually plays in specifically political learning remains. How important is the family in the overall process of political socialization? What conditions determine the amount of influence the family will have in shaping the political learning of its offspring?

The importance of the family relative to other agents of political socialization has become a controversial issue. Early students of political socialization, often taking their cues from work in the area of more general socialization, tended to state boldly that the family was singly the most important agent in political learning. It was regarded as the paramount institution through which political information and outlooks were transmitted from one generation to another, and it provided the context in which political outlooks of emerging citizens were formed. A quotation from a 1965 article by James C. Davies represents this position:

> The family provides the major means for transforming the mentally naked infant organism into the adult, fully clothed in its own personality. And most of the individual's political personality — his tendency to think and act politically in particular ways — have been determined at home, several years before he can take part in politics as an ordinary adult citizen or as a political prominent.[3]

[3] James C. Davies, "The Family's Role in Political Socialization," *The Annals of the American Academy of Political and Social Science*, CCCLXI (September 1955), p. 11.

Some students of political learning have come to question assertions about the dominant role of the family. In a 1972 article that reviewed the evidence on the role of the American family in political socialization R. W. Connell says:

> To sum up: it appears from a substantial body of evidence that processes within the family have been largely irrelevant to the formation of specific opinions. It appears that older and younger generations have developed their opinions in parallel rather than in series, by experiences in a common way of life.[4]

Some have argued that other agents such as the schools are more influential than the family in contemporary American society.[5]

There are merits both to arguments that stress the primacy of the family and those that play down its impact. Rather than try to resolve the question of whether the family is relatively more or less important than other agents, let us ask what political outlooks are more and less likely to be influenced by the family and what factors determine how much of an impact the family will have. In approaching these issues it is useful to consider separately two different forms of socialization: (1) the family as a transmitter of political outlooks, and (2) the family as a shaper of the development of the political self.

THE FAMILY AS A TRANSMITTER OF POLITICAL OUTLOOKS

One approach to the impact of the family in political learning has focused on the direct transmission of particular political outlooks from parent to offspring. For the most part this line of inquiry has looked at the degree of correspondence in the political outlooks between individuals and their parents, or between parents and their offspring. The assumption has been that when parents and their offspring share particular political outlooks one can presume these outlooks have been

[4] R. W. Connell, "Political Socialization and the American Family: The Evidence Re-Examined," *Public Opinion Quarterly,* 36 (1972).

[5] See, for example, Robert Hess and Judith Torney, *The Development of Political Attitudes in Children* (Chicago: Aldine, 1967).

transmitted from parent to offspring. Where such correspondence is not apparent it is presumed that the family is not successfully passing on political outlooks to its offspring, and thus, the family impact is not very great.

Over the past few decades numerous studies have measured and interpreted parent-offspring correspondence in political outlooks. A variety of research techniques have been used. Different types of political outlooks have been investigated. These investigations have found great variations in the extent of parent-offspring congruence.[6] Some have found high levels of correspondence, and others report almost no relationship. Some have found high correspondence for some outlooks but little for others. This variety of findings has led to contradictory assertions about the influence of the family.

Despite the lack of consistency it is possible to make distinctions based on these findings and to suggest patterns of family influence. Given our understanding of how political learning progresses and when and why the family impact is likely to be most apparent, we might expect the family to be more successful in transmitting some types of political outlooks than others. We suggest the following distinctions to interpret the role of the family in transmitting political outlooks.

Basic Political Outlooks and Identities. The family plays its most significant transmission role with respect to those orientations identified in Chapter III as basic political attachments and loyalties. Studies of elementary children have found that many important basic political identities have been formed by the time the child enters school.[7] These identities appear to be formed within the context of the family. This is true of

---

[6] In recent years there has been considerable discussion about the validity of the earlier family transmission studies. See, Connell, *op. cit.;* Richard G. Niemi, "Collecting Information About the Family: A Problem in Survey Methodology," in Jack Dennis (ed.), *Socialization to Politics: A Reader* (New York: Wiley, 1973); and Kent L. Tedin, "The Influence of Parents on the Political Attitudes of Adolescents," *American Political Science Review,* LXVIII (December 1974), pp. 1579–1592.

[7] See Fred I. Greenstein, *Children and Politics* (New Haven: Yale University Press, 1965); and Robert D. Hess and Judith V. Torney, *The Development of Political Attitudes in Children* (Chicago: Aldine, 1967).

identity with the nation, one of the most fundamental political orientations.

Outlooks and identifications regarding ethnic, racial, religious, social class, and regional groupings, as well as certain basic political attachments, are acquired at an early age. They, too, are transmitted by the family. One of the significant roles performed by the family is passing on a set of social identifications and feelings through which the maturing individual forms relationships with the political and social world. The evidence is that these types of political orientations tend to be developed early, persisted in long, and that they are transmitted, at least initially, through the family.[8] In many instances these identities are subsequently reinforced and bolstered by continuing family relationships.

Other basic political predispositions also seem to be transmitted to the child by the family. Although concrete evidence is limited it seems that the family is also important in passing on initial feelings regarding political authorities, as well as the tendency to comply with rules and the wishes of those in positions of authority.[9]

Partisan attachment also seems to be transmitted from parent to offspring. Because of its early acquisition and its persistence as a political reference point, political party attachment is an important political identity for many Americans. Few political orientations have been investigated as extensively in the United States as party identification. Numerous studies have attempted to measure the level of parent-offspring correspondence in partisan attachments. With surprising consistency (given the variety of findings with respect to other political outlooks), investigations have found high congruence for party affiliation. Parent-offspring congruence has been found in studies done on individuals at different points in the life cycle. Adult Americans tend to report that their parents had (have) the same party identification as they report for

[8] See the discussion of this in Chapter IV.

[9] See Robert Weissberg, *Political Learning, Political Choice and Democratic Citizenship* (Englewood Cliffs, N.J.: Prentice-Hall, 1974), pp. 151–153.

themselves.[10] College students also seem to share party identification with their parents.[11] A comprehensive study of American high school seniors found a high level of parent-child correspondence with respect to party identification and support for particular political leaders.[12] Although parent-offspring congruence is not perfect, the level of correspondence and the consistency of findings in this area are impressive. Even those who find little support for the proposition that the family plays an important role in transmitting political outlooks acknowledge the impact of the family with respect to partisan outlooks.[13]

Specific Issue Attitudes and Preferences. The consistently high levels of parent-offspring correspondence found for party identification and the role of the family in transmitting basic political and social identities are not always apparent with respect to more specific issue attitudes and preferences. Lacking comparable data for other issue areas, early students of political socialization often generalized the findings for party identification to other outlooks. What was true for party identification was assumed to be true for other political orientations. This assumption has been found unwarranted. Nor are there good theoretical reasons to assume that the family should be equally influential in passing on attitudes with respect to particular issue questions.

The most comprehensive study of the transmission role of the family is that of M. Kent Jennings and Richard Niemi. Questionnaires were administered to a national sample of high school seniors and to at least one parent of most of the high school students. The authors explored extensively the degree of parent-offspring correspondence across a wide range of political outlooks. Their findings with respect to party

[10] See, for example, Angus Campbell, Gerald Gurin, and Warren E. Miller, *The Voter Decides* (New York: Harper & Row, 1954), p. 99.

[11] R. Middleton and S. Putney, "Student Rebellion Against Parental Political Beliefs," *Social Forces,* 41 (1963), pp. 484–492.

[12] M. Kent Jennings and Richard G. Niemi, *The Political Character of Adolescence* (Princeton: Princeton University Press, 1974), pp. 37–62.

[13] *Ibid.,* and Connell, *loc. cit.*

identification and candidate preferences were mentioned above. Data from that study showing the level of correspondence between parent and offspring for four specific issues are presented in Table VII.1.[14] Note the variation across the four issues. Parent-offspring correspondence is relatively high with respect to the question of "Federal Role in School Integration." On the issue of whether speeches against churches should be permitted, the opinions of the high school seniors are independent of the position of the parent. Regardless of whether parents favored permitting antichurch speeches, the high school seniors endorsed such a right in overwhelming numbers. The data do not indicate that opinions on this issue were passed on to the students by their parents.

In interpreting these relationships one should note that parent-offspring correspondence for each of these four specific issues is less than that found for political party identification in the same study.[15] Parents seem more apt to transmit partisan attachments than positions on specific issues. It is interesting that a similar pattern was found with respect to religious outlooks. There was a high level of parent-offspring congruence with respect to identification with a religious group. However, when one moved from group or institutional preference to specific religious doctrines the correspondence between parent and offspring was considerably lower. Taken together with the patterns regarding political outlooks, these findings suggest that parents are more apt to pass on basic attachments than specific preferences.

The findings from the Jennings and Niemi study of high school seniors and their parents are consistent with the findings of others who have considered parent-offspring congruence over a wide range of political outlooks. R. W. Connell concludes his "reexamination" of the evidence of parental transmission by saying: "That children may gain from their parents some idea of the range of acceptable opinions is quite likely. That specific opinions generally come with

---

[14] Jennings and Niemi, *op. cit.*, p. 78.
[15] Jennings and Niemi report a correlation coefficient of $t_b = 0.47$ with respect to parent-adolescent correspondence for party identification, *Ibid.*, p. 39.

TABLE VII.1 Relationship between Student and Parent Opinions on Four Policy Issues

Students	Federal Role in School Integration [a] Parents			Prayers in Public Schools [a] Parents			Elected Communist Can Hold Office Parents			Allow Speeches against Churches Parents		
	Pro	Depends	Con	Pro	Depends	Con	Pro	Depends [b]	Con	Pro	Depends [b]	Con
Pro	83%	64%	45%	74%	62%	34%	45%	—	32%	88%	—	82%
Depends	7	17	14	3	8	7	1	—	0	0	—	0
Con	10	18	41	23	30	59	53	—	67	12	—	18
Total	100% (961)	99% (202)	100% (453)	100% (1253)	100% (68)	100% (238)	99% (528)	—	99% (1337)	100% (1376)	—	100% (523)
	$\tau_b = .34$			$\tau_b = .29$			$\tau_b = .13$			$\tau_b = .08$		

Source: M. Kent Jennings and Richard G. Niemi, "Relationship between Student and Parent Opinions on Four Policy Issues," in *The Political Character of Adolescence: The Influence of Families and Schools*, p. 78. Copyright © 1974 by Princeton University Press. Reprinted by permission of Princeton University Press.

a Based on pairs in which both the parent and student were "interested enough" to give a pro or con response.

b Ten or fewer cases.

mother's milk is — for America 1944–1968 — rather decisively disproved." [16]

These findings might be disappointing to those who expect (or want) to find across-the-board family transmission of political outlooks, and for those who might be more comfortable with greater consistency across different types of outlooks. However, the findings are not inconsistent with other points we have made about political socialization. The basic political outlooks and attachments for which parental transmission is greatest are the orientations that tend to be acquired early in life, at the point when the impact of the family looms particularly large. Inasmuch as positions on specific issues are formed throughout life, including points in time and in contexts far removed from the early years when the family impact is so strong, it is not surprising that the imprint of the family is less apparent. Issues for which early family positions have little relevance may confront the adult. Other agents of socialization will have had a chance to exert influence by the time the adult citizen, and maybe even the high school senior, forms preferences on specific political issues. The question of permitting antichurch speeches (an outlook for which Jennings and Niemi find little evidence of family opinion transmission), is one not likely to be discussed in the normal course of family life. Parents are not likely to "educate" their offspring or even articulate their own position on this issue. It is more likely to be a topic of discussion in a school civics course or in some other place in the school curriculum.

CONDITIONS AFFECTING THE FAMILY TRANSMISSION OF POLITICAL OUTLOOKS

Even as the family cannot be expected to play an equal role in the transmission of all types of political outlooks, all families cannot be expected to be equally influential in transmitting political attitudes. Even in areas where the parent-offspring correspondent has been found to be high (e.g., party identification), the relationship is not perfect. Not all parents pass their partisan preferences to their offspring. What factors condition

[16] Connell, *op. cit.*, p. 333.

how much influence a family is likely to have? We suggest three important conditions: (1) the existence and articulation of political positions on the part of the parents, (2) the consistency of parental outlooks, and (3) the relationship between the offspring and parents.

Parental Articulation of Political Attitudes. Much of the discussion of the family role in socialization emphasizes why the family is in a position to have an impact. Being in a position to influence and actually making an impact, however, are two different things. Parents may not have opinions themselves. Or they may have them, but make no attempt to communicate them to their children. As we suggested above, politics has little salience for many adults. Discussion of politics and concern for transmitting political outlooks are of little importance to the life of most families. It is reasonable to anticipate that parent-offspring correspondence would not be high when children do not know what positions their parents take on various issues. The more the child knows about parental positions, the more importance parents put on their position on those issues, and the more effort parents make to influence their offspring with respect to those issues, the more impact the family will have in the transmission of political outlooks.

A recent study of high school seniors analyzed these relationships.[17] Like the Jennings and Niemi study this investigation explored the level of congruence between high school students and their parents for a variety of political issues. Taking up the controversial issue of how effective parents are in transmitting specific issue positions, Kent Tedin asked whether successful transmission is related to the accuracy of the adolescent's perception of parental position and the salience of particular issues for the parent. The following hypotheses were posed:

  1. The more accurate the adolescent's perception of the parent's attitudes, the more influence the parent will have on the adolescent's attitude.

[17] Tedin, *loc. cit.*

2. The greater the issue and partisan salience to the parent, the more influence the parent will have on the adolescent's attitude.[18]

Data from the study support both of these hypotheses. See the data presented in Table VII.2.

The data at the top of the table suggest that whether or not students know their parents' positions on the issues makes a difference for their tendency to hold the same position. Among students who were uncertain about parental stands, correspondence between parent and student offspring was negligible. Among those students with accurate perceptions of parental stands, the correspondences were quite high. These findings suggest that political opinions, even on specific issues, get transmitted from parent to offspring when the offspring knows what the parental position is. Conversely, when the adolescents do not know what the parental attitude is, their opinions seem quite independent of their parents. We suggested earlier that parents are more successful in passing on party identification than preferences on specific issues. With this in mind, it is interesting that in Tedin's study the high school seniors were decidedly more likely to have an accurate perception of parental party attachment than the stand of the parent on any of four specific issues. Seventy-two percent of the high school seniors were able to accurately identify parental party identification. No more than 36 percent had an accurate perception of parental preference on any single issue.[19] It is the greater knowledge of the parents' partisan position that accounts for the high correspondence that most studies have found between parents' and offspring party identification. Likewise the relatively greater ignorance of parental stands on other issues helps account for the relatively lower congruence for various specific issues.

A similar pattern is apparent when the relative salience of these issues for the parents is taken into account. Students were considerably more likely to share parental positions on the issues when the parent indicated that the issue was important and that he or she had attempted to communicate that to

18 *Ibid.*, pp. 1579–1592.
19 *Ibid.*, pp. 1585–1586.

TABLE VII.2 *Selected Correlations to Show the Influence of Parents on the Political Attitudes of High School Seniors*

1. Product-Moment Correlations [a] Between Parents and Students on Three Issues Plus Party Identification

Issue	Correlation
Racial integration	.32
China policy	.27
Marijuana laws	.40
Party identification	.48

Interpretation: Moderate to strong correlation between student and parent attitudes; highest correlation is for party identification.

2. Product-Moment Correlations Controlling for Students' Perceptual Accuracy About Parent's Position

Issue	Uncertain	Medium accuracy	Accurate
Racial integration	−.15	.30	.56
China policy	−.08	.21	.51
Marijuana laws	.12	.25	.60
Party identification	.01	—	.57

Interpretation: The more accurate the perceptions students have of their parents' position, the more likely they are to hold the same position.

3. Parent-Adolescent Attitude and Partisan Correlations Within Categories of Issue and Partisan Salience to the Parent

Issue	Low	Medium	High
Racial integration	.00	.27	.48
China policy	.03	.25	.44
Marijuana laws	−.21	.35	.48
	Independent	Weak attachment	Strong attachment
Party identification	.28	.31	.68

Interpretation: The more salient an issue is to the parent, the more likely the student is to hold the same position as the parent.

Source: Kent L. Tedin, "The Influence of Parents on the Political Attitudes of Adolescents," *American Political Science Review LXVII* (December 1974), pp. 1584, 1586, 1587. Reprinted by permission of the American Political Science Association.

the child. Data demonstrating these relationships are also presented at the bottom of Table VII.2. When parents indicated that the issue was of low salience, relationships between parental and student opinions on that issue were extremely low. For the marijuana issue the relationship was even somewhat negative (i.e., there was a slight tendency for the student to have an opinion opposite that of his or her parents when the issue was not salient for the parents). However, when the parents indicated an issue was salient for them, the parent-offspring correspondence was considerably higher. Tedin rejects the proposition that parents are not capable of transmitting positions on particular issues:

> In recent years, students of political socialization have downplayed the family as a source of attitudes toward public issues. This conclusion is not unwarranted given the data. But it would seem not to be an inherent characteristic of parent-child attitude transmission. Rather, quite the opposite appears to be the case. Parents have an inherent potential for successful transmission. Whether this potential is realized depends basically on the distribution within the population of (1) issue salient to the parent, and (2) adolescent perceptual accuracy of the parent attitude.[20]

Parents are in a position to have more impact in transmitting political outlooks than they exercise. In general, politics is not of high salience to most parents and positions on political issues are not considered to be particularly relevant for relationships within the family. When the parents have positions on issues, make their positions known to their offspring, and indicate concern for the positions taken by their offspring, parents have considerable influence in shaping the political

[20] *Ibid.*, p. 1592.

a These correlation coefficients indicate the level of association between the issue positions of students and their parents. The higher the number, the greater the agreement between student and parents. A coefficient of .00 indicates no relationship exists — i.e., parents do not pass on their positions to their offspring. The closer the coefficient is to 1.00, the higher is the student-parent agreement. A minus sign indicates an inverse, or negative, relationship — i.e., the tendency is for parents and offspring to have different positions.

positions of their offspring. When parents fail to do these things specific opinions are less likely to be transmitted. In the absence of parental influence other socializing influences can come into play.

Parental Agreement. The extent to which parents agree on political positions also seems relevant for the transmission of parental attitudes. Although there is a tendency for parents to have similar viewpoints on political issues, mothers and fathers do not always take the same position. How does parental agreement or disagreement affect the impact of the family in shaping political outlooks? In cases of parental disagreement are the offspring more likely to follow the lead of the father or the mother?

Agreement between parents on political issues seems to affect the ability of the parents to transmit their position to their offspring. The impact of a particular parent on the child or youth is greatly strengthened when it is reinforced by the other parent. Conversely, the influence of one parent is diminished when the other parent takes a different position. After an analysis of the impact of parental agreement on parent-offspring transmission over a wide range of political outlooks, Jennings and Niemi conclude:

> Almost without exception the child is more likely to reflect one parent's orientation when that orientation is also shared by the other parent. Similarly, the child is less likely to reproduce one parent's orientation when that orientation is not shared by the other parent.[21]

Jennings and Niemi also found that when parents differed the adolescent student was somewhat more likely to agree with the position of the mother rather than that of the father. Despite the fact that males are generally seen as the dominant figure when it comes to politics, the child seems more likely to take the political lead of the mother.[22]

Relationships between Parent and Offspring. We pointed out above that one of the factors that contributes to the po-

[21] Jennings and Niemi, *op. cit.*
[22] *Ibid.*

tential impact of the family in shaping the outlooks of its offspring is the strength of personal ties established in the context of the family. The level of positive affective ties is not the same within all families. Some offspring, especially as they reach adolescence and adulthood, may develop less close ties and even negative feelings regarding their parents. We would expect more parent-offspring correspondence in political outlooks when relationships between parent and offspring are close and positive.

This relationship has been investigated in several studies. Although the evidence is not fully consistent the bulk of it supports the proposition. Tedin found that parent-adolescent agreement was enhanced on most political outlooks when the adolescents reported feeling "close" to the parent and "admired" the parent.[23] Jennings and Niemi found that the impact of the quality of parent-adolescent relationships was more apparent with respect to specific policy issues than for partisan attachments.[24] Herbert McClosky and H. E. Dahlgren found that closeness of family ties affected partisan attachments even among adults.[25]

Several studies have found that parental-offspring correspondence is affected by the amount and type of control that parents exert over their children. Parent-offspring correspondence seems to be highest in cases where the offspring report medium amounts of parental control or what they judge to be the right amount of control. Those who report either low or high levels of parental control seem to be less likely to share political outlooks with their parents.[26]

THE FAMILY AS SHAPER OF POLITICAL SELF
DEVELOPMENT

The direct transmission of political outlooks from parent to offspring is only one way the family influences political learn-

[23] Tedin, *op. cit.*, pp. 1587–1588.

[24] Jennings and Niemi, *op. cit.*

[25] Herbert McClosky and H. E. Dahlgren, "Primary Group Influence on Party Loyalty," *American Political Science Review*, LIII (1963), pp. 757–776.

[26] For a review of research findings on this, see David Sears, "Political Socialization," in Fred I. Greenstein and Nelson Polsby (eds.), *Handbook of Political Science*, Vol. 2 (Reading, Mass.: Addison-Wesley, 1975), p. 126.

ing. The family also socializes its offspring into political life as it shapes outlooks such as self-evaluations, personality, and personal and social values, which are often relevant for the development of more specifically political outlooks; and as it provides a context in which the development of political thinking take place.[27] To some extent the two contradictory evaluations of family impact cited above (that by Davies stressing the dominant role of the family and that by Connell suggesting that existent evidence does not support the assertion that the family plays a crucial role in transmitting political outlooks) entail different conceptions of political socialization.[28] Connell deals with the transmission of specific political attitudes. Davies looks at the development of basic outlooks and needs that determine how the maturing individual will relate to the political world. It is possible for one to hold that the family is not very successful in transmitting specific political positions to its offspring and still claim that it plays a prominent role in political learning; inasmuch as it is crucial for shaping predispositions that determine how the individual relates to the political world. This constitutes the core of what we have referred to as indirect political socialization.

Studies specifically analyzing this mode of family impact are rarer and less conclusive than those dealing with the family transmission of specific political outlooks. A number of theories and studies indicate the crucial role of the family in determining basic personality, individual self-concepts, and social values and identifications. Evidence linking these personal traits and predispositions to more specifically political outlooks, however, is still somewhat sparse and controversial. Conceptually and methodologically this remains one of the messier areas in the analysis of political behavior.[29] One factor that has made good evidence on the impact of more personal aspects of individual development less available is the fact that indirect political learning is less relevant for the

[27] See Richard M. Merelman, "The Development of Political Ideology: A Framework for the Analysis of Political Socialization," *American Political Science Review*, LXIII (1969), pp. 750–767.

[28] This distinction was suggested in the beginning of Chapter VI.

[29] For a review of literature relating personality to political outlooks and behavior, see Fred I. Greenstein, "Personality and Politics," in Greenstein and Polsby, *op. cit.*, pp. 1–92.

types of political orientations that are easy to identify and measure. Partisan identification, preferences for particular political leaders, positions on specific issues, and voting regularity are relatively easy to tap through opinion surveys. These are not the orientations most likely to be related in a causal way to personal predispositions. They are more likely to be picked up through direct teaching and imitation. Personality and self-perceptions are more likely to be related to political predispositions such as a sense of political competence or efficacy, a tendency to follow political leaders rather than form opinions independently, and general predispositions toward trust and respect for those in positions of authority.[30] Gabriel Almond and Sidney Verba, in their comparative study of political cultures in five nations, found evidence that a sense of civic competence is related to more general feelings of self-competence.[31] They also found that the ability to participate in making decisions and to question parental authorities in the family during the childhood years was related to having a sense of civic competence in later years.

The family influences political learning in yet another sense. One important aspect of political learning involves the development of political thinking and consciousness. To a considerable extent the atmosphere within the family, relationships among family members, and the types of stimulation the children receive help to shape the development of political thinking. Richard M. Merelman has paid particular attention to this aspect of political socialization, especially with respect to the development of moral and ideological thinking. He argues that there is a link between positive identification between offspring and parents and the development of moral and cognitive skills.[32] These, in turn, are related to the capacity to think about politics. Positive forms of identification encourage the growth of political ideology in the maturing child.[33]

The family influences and gives shape to the development

[30] See Gabriel Almond and Sidney Verba, *The Civic Culture* (Princeton: Princeton University Press, 1963), especially ch. 12.

[31] *Ibid.*, ch. 8.

[32] Merelman, *loc. cit.*

[33] *Ibid.*, pp. 758–764.

of the political self in a number of different ways. Even the family that is not much concerned about politics and makes no effort to pass political outlooks on to its offspring is likely to influence the development of political thinking. It is not likely that one's family will leave no imprint upon one's particular political world.

SUMMARY: THE FAMILY IN POLITICAL SOCIALIZATION

In this chapter we have argued that the family is one of the key associations through which political socialization is accomplished. It contributes to political learning in several ways. The major influence of the family is felt in the acquisition of basic political outlooks, including attachments to the system as a whole and identification with political and other social groupings. The family also affects political learning as it has an impact on personal and social outlooks that have relevance for specifically political outlooks and as it contributes to the context in which early political thinking and consciousness are developed. Families are in a position to exert more influence on political learning than they actually do. Politics is not of high salience within most families. Parents often make little effort to articulate their own positions and to push their children toward adopting them. The absence of political education in the family opens the door for other groups and associations to influence political learning — schools, friends, and associations in later life.

Thus far we have considered family influence in terms of the impact of parents upon their offspring during childhood and youth. Although this is the most important form of family impact, the parent to child influence is not the only sequence through which the family shapes and sustains political outlooks. In some instances the parent to offspring flow of influence is reversed. This is particularly true as the offspring reach late adolescence and adulthood. Child to parent influence can be especially important in immigrant families. Through school and other associations the children become socialized into the new society. They in turn, pass on what they have learned to their parents. In this way they help to socialize their parents into the new society. Siblings within the same family also may play roles in political socialization. Older brothers and sisters can serve as important role models and as communicators of political ideas for younger children. As such they help to shape their political development.

Parent-offspring influence often continues beyond childhood and youth. The early years may be the time when parents have their greatest impact. Contact between parent and offspring is most frequent, and the younger generation is in the process of forming their political outlooks. However, the close personal ties that contribute to family impact normally do not cease when the offspring grow up. McClosky and Dahlgren make this point. After an extensive investigation of how the family context contributes to the stability of party loyalty, they conclude: "The family thus serves as a continuing agency for defining party affiliation of its members." [34] The amount of family interaction, the closeness of ties, and the salience of politics for family members continue to condition the family influence throughout the life cycle.

From the standpoint of society, the fact that families serve as major agents of socialization means that the process is not highly centralized and that some of the most influential components of political socialization are beyond the direct manipulation of regime leaders. When a large number of small, somewhat autonomous units carry out some of the most important aspects of political learning, it is difficult for regime leaders to oversee closely the processes and content of political socialization.

The important role of the family also helps to make political learning haphazard and unsystematic. Families, in general, do not perform political socialization as a conscious and deliberate task. Much of the political learning that takes place in the family occurs without systematic planning or intent. Political party affiliation and other political attachments are transferred from parent to offspring, attitudes toward authorities and political action are developed, and positions on issues are acquired within the family context — often as unintended consequences of other family concerns and activities.

[34] McClosky and Dahlgren, *op. cit.*, p. 775.

The important role played by the family, especially in transmitting social and political attachments, contributes to variety in political outlooks. Families differ in their regard for existent political institutions and leaders. Families are tied into different social, economic, religious, ethnic, and regional groups, which often entail particular perspectives on political life. As a result of these varying ties different families pass on different attitudes and evaluations. In this way family socialization serves to perpetuate diversity in social and political viewpoints and can counteract pressures toward centralized socialization and homogeneity in political outlooks — goals sometimes sought by regime leaders. The persistence of partisan attachments or particular political perspectives within geographic regions, among members of specific subgroups, and persons who share a particular position in the socioeconomic structure result, in part, from the tendency of these group-related outlooks to be passed on within a family from one generation to the next.

The important role of the family also tends to give a conservative or preserving bias to political socialization. Families, in part because of their transgenerational makeup, tend to transmit outlooks from the older generation to the younger. Because the children tend to model themselves after their parents and because the parents attempt to recreate themselves in their children, transgenerational influence, more often than not, serves to conserve rather than change. Because of this conservative bias, the family impact on political socialization often works to inhibit rapid and uniform change in mass political outlooks.

CHAPTER VIII

Education, the Schools, and Political Learning

EDUCATION AND SCHOOLING: AN OVERVIEW

Schooling, be it in a jungle, a field, or a classroom, is an experience few children in the world avoid. The years between early childhood and puberty (in nonliterate societies) and between early childhood and late adolescence (in literate societies) are given over in large part to learning the skills and values that prepare the child for adulthood. Instruction may be in the hands of teachers specially appointed to this task, or it may be left to parents or older siblings. The instruction may be organized into regular classes, or it may be in a less explicit program. The schooling may stress reading and writing, food gathering techniques, weapons and fighting, or numerous other technologies and skills. However programmed, and whatever its contents, schooling in the fundamentals of a society's technology is seldom left to chance.[1]

The schooling that provides the child with the fundamentals of his or her society's technology also helps him or her acquire the cultural norms associated with membership in society. We see this clearly in the familiar curriculum of Western schools. Civics classes are taught along with reading

---

[1] Erik H. Erikson has written that all children, in all cultures, must adjust to the inorganic laws of the tool world. See *Childhood and Society* (New York: Norton, 1950), ch. 7.

classes. Good conduct is instilled along with good grammar. The beginning school child learns that obedience to authority is as necessary for success as is conquering the new math. The African herdsboy has a schooling that in its outcome is similar. The rules and regulations governing the care of the cattle are intended not only to guarantee that he knows how to keep cattle, but also to introduce him to an intricate system of cultural norms regarding the social and political life of the community. So it is across the world and through the ages — preadult years are a time for acquiring the tools and learning the rules that pave the way for adulthood.

We are, of course, more interested in the second half of this formula — learning the norms of the society. More narrowly still, we focus on those aspects of schooling that have consequences for political life. To avoid terminological confusion, we distinguish schooling from education.

It is a commonplace that education and schooling are not synonymous. Society educates through a wide variety of agencies — the family, the clan elders, churches, mass media, ad infinitum. The classroom takes its place alongside these other educational forces. It neither replaces nor dominates them. In this chapter we restrict ourselves to the formal educational system, especially to mass public education systems such as that in the United States.

Allowing for considerable variation between nations, the following elements are common to public education systems:

   1. Tax-supported public institutions explicitly charged with instructing the young in a wide variety of skills and values
   2. Specially trained and recruited personnel to do the teaching
   3. More or less daily attendance during the better part of the years between the ages of six and sixteen
   4. A more or less common curriculum so children of the same age receive fairly similar instruction

This is, of course, a Western picture, although one not unfamiliar to African, Asian, and Latin American students. Important exceptions appear as one shifts from country to country. Some states charge school fees; in other states, the schools are totally free. In most nations there are private and parochial educational systems in addition to the public schools. These, however, are apt to follow a similar general format. Different proportions of the school-age populations of different nations are actually in school. Less than 5 percent of Uganda's adolescents, for example, are in secondary schools, compared with 95 percent of young people in the United States. The school curriculum in France is much more uniform than that of India, where even the language of instruction varies from area to area.

In most societies the school years begin at age five or six and end at seventeen or eighteen, except for the few who continue with higher education. As we have shown in previous chapters, these years are critical for the development of the political self. We try here to show how schools socialize young people politically. The reader should keep in mind two qualifications. First, the major agencies discussed elsewhere — the family and social groups — operate concurrently with the school as political socialization forces. Although during the first few years in the individual's life the family has almost exclusive influence, schools seldom have such a monopoly of access. Schools may or may not teach the same values as other socializing agents. Second, the years between five and eighteen cover considerable ground, especially in respect to the formation of the political self. Frequently we are forced to speak of the "school years" or "school experiences" without distinguishing between elementary and high school. The reader should bear in mind the ideas presented in previous chapters about the differential rate and content of political socialization for different age groups.

We discuss the school in political socialization with respect to: (1) the influence of the classroom, focusing on the formal curriculum, the ritual life, and the teacher; and (2) aspects of the school other than the formal classroom: the social climate of the school, political youth organizations, and extracurricular activities.

THE FORMAL CLASSROOM AND POLITICAL SOCIALIZATION

In modern societies political learning is expected to take place in the classroom. It is here that comprehensive and deliberate efforts are made by modern and modernizing polities to shape the political outlooks of new citizens. Within the classroom the formal curriculum of instruction, various ritual activities, and the activities of the teacher all affect the political development of youngsters.

THE CURRICULUM

The curriculum is potentially one of the major instruments of political socialization. Its importance as an initiator and reinforcer of cultural values is well stated by C. Arnold Anderson and Suellen Fisher:

> The school curriculum that lies in the heart of the educational systems of western societies is one of the great cultural forms of human history. Its content embraces diverse culture traits believed to be requisite for participation in the society. . . . Many of the basic "values" of the society are to be reinforced (if not originally transmitted to pupils) by means of the choice of materials placed before them in society.[2]

Nationalistic values, in particular, permeate the curriculum. Courses in national history tend to be selective: "those episodes that redound most to our national glory receive emphasis; and the picture of the past is deficient in cracks and crevices."[3] Formal instruction in civics and government is designed to acquaint the adolescent citizen with the nature and the glory of the established order. The use of literature reflects favorably on the nation's past and forecasts great things for its future. Such portrayals are presented for citizenship training. Generally political leaders and educators explicitly view the curriculum as an appropriate agency for transmitting knowledge and values conducive to good citizenship.

A distinction can be made between two types of political instruction: civic education and political indoctrination. The distinction is ambiguous, but will serve the purpose at hand.

---

[2] C. Arnold Anderson and Suellen Fisher, "The Curriculum as an Instrument for Inculcating Attitudes and Values," Comparative Education Center, University of Chicago, unpublished manuscript, 1967.

[3] V. O. Key, Jr., *Public Opinion and American Democracy* (New York: Knopf, 1961), p. 317.

Following the suggestion of James Coleman, we call *civic training* that part of political education that emphasizes how a good citizen participates in the political life of his or her nation. *Political indoctrination* concerns the learning of a specific political ideology intended to rationalize and justify a particular regime.[4] Civic training acquaints the student with the nation toward which loyalty is assumed. Political indoctrination inculcates loyalty to the nation. In Chapter II we discussed censorship and propaganda, which are aspects of political indoctrination. When groups in control of society fear their authority is ebbing, they stress censorship (keeping citizens from learning things that might further erode authority, as when Nixon tried to keep the White House tapes private) and propaganda (insisting that citizens hear things that justify the acts of groups in power).

What to call civic education and what to call political indoctrination always depends somewhat on the political values of whoever is doing the labeling. A school lesson celebrating the free enterprise economy would be viewed as civic education by the Chamber of Commerce, but as political indoctrination by the Socialist-Labor party. Admitting the difficulty of classification, it is still useful to look at school curricula from the perspective of both civic education and political indoctrination.

Civic Training. In an early classic study, *The Making of Citizens,* Charles Merriam observed that:

> The school emerges in recent times as the major instrument in the shaping of civic education. A process, extending over a considerable period of years, now takes the place of the week or ten days once given to the tribal candidate in his period of novitiate, and organizes and schematizes this process with great elaboration. With the development of universal education, the training is extended to the entire population, female as well as male, and the whole community is drawn into the net.[5]

[4] See James S. Coleman (ed.), *Education and Political Development* (Princeton: Princeton University Press, 1965), p. 226.

[5] Charles E. Merriam, *The Making of Citizens* (Chicago: The University of Chicago Press, 1931), p. 273.

Merriam summarized the findings of a survey of eight western nations. He further observed that, "In all the systems appraised in this study, the school emerges as the heart of the civic education of the political community, and in all probability will continue to function increasingly in this role." [6]

Educators, students of politics, journalists, and others have echoed Merriam for the last four and a half decades. There is no doubt that citizenship training is a part of most school curricula. There is some doubt about the influence of such programs. Some commentators, sensitive to the gap between what is taught in the school and what the child learns outside the classroom, play down the influence of such attempts at civic training.

An anthropological study of Peyrane, a French village in the Vaucluse, is worth citing in this context. [7] Laurence Wylie reports that the local school has various civics courses. Students memorize sentences that stress the benevolent, disinterested nature of the government. But parents and teachers speak a different language when they talk about the government. The attitude taught when the children overhear adults "is in direct conflict with what the children are taught in school." [8] From listening to the grownups, children learn that government is made up of "weak, stupid, selfish, ambitious men." [9] No matter what image the children read about in their civics textbooks, they "constantly hear adults referring to Government as a source of evil and to the men who run it as instruments of evil." [10] They further learn that it is the "duty of the citizen *not* to cooperate with these men, as the civic books would have people do, but rather to hinder them, to prevent them in every possible way from increasing their power over individuals and over families." [11] The content of the formal school curriculum is probably superseded by informal learning experiences.

[6] *Ibid.,* p. 288.
[7] Laurence Wylie, *Village in the Vaucluse* (Cambridge, Mass.: Harvard University Press, 1957).
[8] *Ibid.,* p. 206.
[9] *Ibid.,* p. 207.
[10] *Ibid.,* p. 208.
[11] *Ibid.,* p. 207.

For most students the discrepancy between curriculum materials and other political cues is not as severe. When the textbook portrays a political world confirmed by his or her own observation, or by what is transmitted by other socialization agents, the student will be more receptive to its political lessons. A study of civic training in several American high schools confirms this notion.[12] This study found that the curriculum did affect the kinds of political values developed by students. The influence was accelerated when the values being taught were in harmony with those articulated by other socialization agents. It was attenuated, however, where the textbook values were out of line with the norms of other, more powerful, agents of political learning.

In another study, the authors reported that American high school students taking civics courses differ only marginally from students not enrolled in such courses.[13] At best, attending a class in American government leads to incremental increases in a student's level of political information, his sense of political effectiveness, his feeling of patriotism, or his propensity to be a political participant. This study is consistent with material presented earlier; the American high-school student is already socialized with respect to many political attributes by this stage in his life. Civics courses have little influence.

The few studies linking curriculum to the formation of political orientations are more suggestive than definitive. Their findings vary. It seems clear, however, that in the absence of formal civic education, members of society would be less informed about the political world. They would have less information concerning their political structures and processes. It is doubtful, however, that basic political loyalties and attachments are substantially developed or altered through such formal civic education. If the civic training in the curriculum

[12] Edgar Litt, "Civic Education, Community Norms, and Political Indoctrination," *American Sociological Review*, XXVIII (1963), pp. 69–75. Reprinted in Litt (ed.), *The Political Imagination* (Glenview, Ill.: Scott, Foresman, 1966), pp. 487–494.

[13] Kenneth P. Langton and M. Kent Jennings, "Political Socialization and the High School Civics Curriculum in the United States," *American Political Science Review*, 62 (September 1968), pp. 852–867.

is inconsistent with what is learned about the political world from adults, peer groups, and other agents of political socialization, it may not be very effective.

Political Indoctrination. All school systems carry on some form of political indoctrination. The myths and legends from the past, the policies and programs of the present, and the goals and aspirations of the future are taught selectively. Consciously or not, textbooks and other teaching materials justify and rationalize political practices. The goals and means of political indoctrination through classroom materials, however, are more obvious in some nations than in others. Children in different nations receive varying doses of slanted material. Political authorities permit varying degrees of honest criticism to appear in course materials.

The Soviet Union has been identified by both popular opinion and scholars as a nation that engages in considerable political indoctrination. Frederick C. Barghoorn writes that: "The Soviet leaders seek to shape communication and personal relationships in school, family and other attitude-forming institutions so as to inculcate the maximum possible devotion to the polity." [14] The Soviet principles of pedagogy, first formulated in the 1930s, accept as their aim "the formation of behavior, character, and traits of personality necessary to the Soviet state." [15] The most important teaching agent has been the schools. Indeed, according to Jeremy Azrael, the chief goal of the educational experience has been to inculcate "loyalty and support for the polity, its leaders and their policies." [16] A major part of this indoctrination is done through the curriculum. Ideological considerations have led to the politicization of the entire curriculum, with the heaviest burden being placed on the social sciences and humanities. Songbooks, readers, and textbooks have been designed to convince students that the accomplishments of the Soviet people in sci-

[14] Frederick I. Barghoorn, *Politics in the USSR* (Boston: Little, Brown, 1966), p. 84.

[15] Quoted by Barghoorn, *ibid.,* p. 85, from N. A. Lyalin (ed.), *Kollektiv i razvitie lichnosti shkolnika* (Leningrad, 1962), p. 28.

[16] Jeremy R. Azrael, "Soviet Union," in Coleman, *op. cit.,* p. 237.

ence and art, in agriculture and industry, are unequaled anywhere in the world.

The Soviet Union is not the only instance of extensive use of school curricula for political indoctrination. Richard Fagen has translated an arithmetic workbook used in Cuban schools for worker and peasant education that has many examples of such curriculum manipulation. One of the more suggestive problem exercises goes like this:

> Imperialism knows no other type of relations between States except domination and subjugation, the oppression of the weak by the strong. It bases international relations on abuse and threat, on violence and arbitration.
>
> Between January 3 and June 10 in 1961, North American military airplanes violated Cuban airspace 3 times in the month of January, 15 in February, 17 in March, 9 in April, 8 in May, and 10 in June. What was the average monthly number of violations of Cuban air space by North American military airplanes? [17]

The kibbutz experiments in Israeli education afford another example of how a curriculum can be permeated by a national ideology. In his study of child training on a kibbutz, Melford Spiro quotes a paragraph from a statement describing the educational philosophy:

> The aims which express our *weltanschauung* should be expressed in every study-project, in every discussion, and in every socio-cultural activity. In every subject — nature, the Homeland, Bible, economics — one should uncover the political causes that are concealed in these subjects: criticism of society, social justice, existence of social classes, national oppression, exile and suffering of Jews. . . .

From his observations of classroom discussions, Spiro concludes that many discussions are "ideological indoctrination which are labeled . . . as scientific truth rather than ideology." [18]

In one context or another all nations indulge in some form

[17] Richard R. Fagen, *Cuba: The Political Content of Adult Education* (Stanford: The Hoover Institution of War and Peace, 1964), p. 68.

[18] Melford E. Spiro, *Children of the Kibbutz* (New York: Schocken Books, 1965), p. 257.

of political indoctrination through textbooks and classroom materials. The existence of such efforts can be easily documented. However, knowing that a school's curriculum includes a certain type of lesson tells us little about its impact. Teaching a particular value in a classroom is not presumptive evidence that the value is internalized by the student. Students rarely become perfect replicas of the model citizen portrayed in political indoctrination. In some instances political indoctrination efforts in the classroom, like some attempts as civic education, may be quite ineffective, boring students rather than instructing them.

CLASSROOM RITUAL LIFE

Political values are also transmitted to the child through the ritual life of the classroom — saluting the flag, singing patriotic songs, honoring national heroes and events, and being exposed to patriotic symbols such as pictures and sayings of leaders. With greater or lesser self-consciousness, schools throughout the world append to the normal curriculum numerous ceremonial expressions of devotion to the nation. Educational policy makers assume that systematic exposure to such symbols will produce greater attachment and respect for the nation and its institutions. Patriotic feelings are formed and cemented by participation in ritual acts.

Indicating the importance placed on ritual exercises is the amount of time and resources allocated to them. Teachers are compelled, by social norms if not always by law, to spend valuable school hours and scarce resources on classroom activities and programs that stress national patriotism. Such investments are made in the overextended school systems of developing nations as well as in more affluent countries. A recent parliamentary debate on educational policy in an African country concluded that copies of the national anthem should be printed and distributed to every school in the nation, including schools suffering from such critical disadvantages as no electricity and no writing materials.

A particularly rich illustration of the ritual life of the school is presented in Herbert Passin's discussion of Imperial

Japan.[19] He writes that the official doctrine of the state was promoted in a variety of ways, not the least of which was the ritual activity expected of every student.

> There were frequent ceremonial assemblies requiring the reading of the Imperial Rescript on Education, the showing of the Imperial Portraits, the raising of the national flag, etc., and these were carried through with the utmost protocol and graveness to make a proper impression on the children. . . . So sacred were these symbols that in case of fire they were to be saved before everything else, even at the risk of life. . . . The cult of the state . . . was brought into close relation with the school system. Its doctrines were taught, and pupils were required to participate in its rituals and visit its shrines on ceremonial and national occasions. Schools organized pilgrimages and outings designed to strengthen the pupils' loyalty and devotion to the national cult.[20]

The fact that ritual experiences are stressed in the classroom and that they are deemed an important part of political indoctrination programs by most regimes, however, does not give a clear picture of what is contained in them, how effective they are, and how important they are in relation to other socialization methods. Evidence on these issues awaits more research. We can, however, suggest two possible implications of the students' ritual life.

First, rituals are the acting out of a sense of awe toward what is symbolized by the ritual. Basic feelings of patriotism and loyalty are reinforced as one acts out devotion to the state. In their report on American school children, Hess and Torney comment: "The feelings of respect for the pledge and the national anthem are reinforced daily and are seldom

[19] Passin describes in some detail the indoctrination efforts of Japanese educational authorities. He questions the effect of the political indoctrination campaigns. "It is clear . . . that there were strong elements of resistance to the penetration of the official doctrine. . . . Nor is there any evidence that the officially promoted morality penetrated as deeply among the masses as the leaders might have hoped. For many people, the official dogmas were mere formalities external to themselves and their way of life." See his "Japan" in Coleman, *ibid.*, pp. 310–311.

[20] *Ibid.*, pp. 308–309.

questioned by the child." [21] The very gestures and words associated with the acts suggest submission, respect, and dependence. The rituals "establish an emotional orientation toward country and flag even though an understanding of the meaning of the words and actions has not been developed. These seem to be indoctrinating acts that cue and reinforce feelings of loyalty and patriotism." [22]

In some instances these ritual experiences in school may reinforce political loyalties that have already been formed in the family; in others they may introduce the child to such orientations. The former pattern is likely to occur in more established polities, and the latter may be a significant phenomenon in newer nations. Either way, such ritual experiences are of great importance. "This early orientation prepares the child for later learning and stresses the importance of loyalty for citizens of all ages." [23]

Second, rituals also emphasize the collective nature of patriotism. Saluting the flag, singing the anthems, and honoring national figures are group activities. Group experiences can be very compelling, especially to the impressionable mind of the child. Consider the difference between the classroom and the family as settings for acquiring emotional attachment to the country. In the family, the child may learn to be patriotic because he or she recognizes that this orientation is highly valued by the adults he or she tries to imitate. Patriotism in the classroom, in contrast, is *acted out* in the rituals, and acted out by the individual in a group he or she has become closely related with. In an attenuated way, the classroom approximates the "we-feeling" that is an important part of the political culture. The rituals lay the groundwork for adult political activity — most of which is necessarily group activity. Nationalism, partisanship, and identification with a social or political movement are orientations more meaningful when

---

[21] Robert D. Hess and Judith V. Torney, *The Development of Political Attitudes in Children* (Chicago: Aldine, 1967), p. 106.
[22] *Ibid.*
[23] *Ibid.*, p. 108.

experienced as part of a collectivity. The ritual life of the school often involves such collective experiences.

THE TEACHER

The third way in which the classroom affects political socialization is through the teacher. Because of the teacher's special role in society and direct contact with youth during their formative years, he or she has considerable influence on the child's political orientations.

First, for the child the teacher represents an authoritative spokesman of society. The teacher is often the first model of political authority the beginning student encounters. How new this kind of authority is to a child can be seen by comparing the parent and the teacher. When a child responds to his parent as an authority figure, he does not separate the role from the incumbent of the role. He keeps the same parent permanently. Consequently, parents are very personal authority figures; they dispense rewards and punishments in what often appear to be idiosyncratic and even capricious ways. The public school teacher as an authority figure, on the other hand, is much more like a political authority. The child learns that the authority role and incumbent of the role are separate factors. He learns he should obey any incumbent who happens to occupy the role "teacher." Further, he discovers that rewards and punishments from authorities are affected by identifiable constraints that operate on the particular person in the role. The teacher, like the policeman, president, or mayor, is part of an institutional pattern, a constitutional order.

In addition to this position of authority in the classroom, the teacher also benefits from a position of general respect and trust in his or her community. Especially in rural areas and villages, people look up to the public school teacher as a repository of knowledge and civilization. In some locations he or she also enjoys prestige as the major representative of the government. In Asian and African villages the teacher is presumptively a community leader in activities ranging far beyond education.

The teacher serves as society's representative and partner in the task of rearing children; he or she is generally respected and is expected to be a model of behavior and of social values. The more important issue here, however, is how and to what degree the teacher affects the political development of his charges. We can inquire into these questions in two ways, by examining the teacher (1) as a holder of specific political values and opinions and a disseminator of such orientations, and (2) as a creator and manipulator of a "learning culture" in the classroom, which has important indirect political consequences.

The Teacher as Disseminator of Political Values. The teacher might express opinions on two different types of political values: consensus values and partisan values. *Consensus values* are those presumably shared throughout society: faith in the American form of government, confidence in the electoral process, commitment to majority rule as well as the protection of minority rights, and so forth. *Partisan values* are those that divide the society: Republicans versus Democrats, policy positions, and so forth.

It is generally assumed that the teacher will give verbal support to consensus values, but will not use the classroom as a forum for discussion of "partisan values" and controversial positions. Democracy, the two-party system, free enterprise, basic freedoms, and so forth, are not only permissible subjects in the classroom; the teacher is expected to urge these beliefs on his students. Liberal or conservative positions, foreign policy views, party allegiances, on the other hand, are seen as partisan values; and the teacher generally is expected to avoid particular interpretations of such issues.

The teacher, then, is expected simultaneously to be very political in some senses, and apolitical in others. The evidence suggests that the American public school teacher is generally adroit in balancing these two demands.

In recent years, however, it has been more difficult for the public school teacher to tread the thin line between "safe" consensus values and "unsafe" partisan values. One reason is that the teachers themselves are more visible political actors, especially with the unionization of teachers and the frequent threat of and even use of teacher strikes. Students can hardly fail to see teachers as partisan political actors when schools are closed by strike activity and the school is surrounded by picket lines.

Further erosion of the apolitical role of the teacher was introduced by the political events of the late 1960s and early 1970s. Partisan politics — civil rights activity, antibussing campaigns, pro-war and antiwar movements — penetrated at least some American high schools, especially urban high schools with racially mixed populations and other high schools in proximity to colleges and universities. Teachers found it more and more difficult to stay aloof from the intense partisan differences of that period. Although student politics have quieted down, the loss of political innocence in the public schools has left its mark.

One obvious change has been the shift from "safe" and uncritical" materials to much more "critical" teaching about American society. Take American history. Traditionally this subject has been taught as a chronological account of past events and American heroes. The standard approach glorified and celebrated the American past. Recently a "new history" has been introduced in classrooms. The new history stresses critical thinking and independent judgment by students. The purpose is to provide students with criteria by which to evaluate how Americans, especially leaders, have behaved in the past. About one-fourth of the nation's 17,000 high schools are using the new history materials.

Patrick Buchanan, a syndicated newspaper columnist, whose writings appear in papers across the nation, spoke out strongly against the new history in an article, "An America Without Heroes." [24] He wrote of a Virginia high school in which eleventh grade students concluded that Thomas Jefferson was a hypocrite and students in an American civilization course believe that Abraham Lincoln was a racist. One graduating senior, Buchanan wrote, viewed the American era of Manifest Destiny in terms of "European dropouts who came over here

[24] This column, a *New York Times* Special Feature, appeared in the *Chicago Tribune,* June 4, 1975.

and just loved to push the Indians around. That made them feel superior."

Buchanan was furious: "It is ludicrous that we should sit still for this. Americans have the right to have their tax-supported schools teach their children not only to revere the great men of America's past, but to understand, respect, appreciate, and defend the society and systems in which Americans have chosen to live." Speaking in language familiar to the student of political socialization, the newspaper columnist insists that, "The mythology, the shared beliefs, the heroes of American history are part of the cement that binds together this diverse society. They are part of the common heritage of all Americans, which every citizen should know."

The Teacher and the Learning Culture. The teacher also affects the political development of the student by establishing some sort of "learning culture" or "social system" in the classroom. The elementary school teacher with whom millions of children the world over have daily contact is institutionally defined as superior to the child. He or she knows more about the subject matter, establishes and interprets school rules, is looked up to as a behavioral model, and is publicly labeled a representative of society's authority over the young. In a normal day the elementary teacher will have more than 10,000 exchanges with the student through which he or she will transmit numerous cultural values. Some of these values, as discussed above, will have specific political content; others will have latent political meaning. As the first person to represent to the child the large, impersonal society beyond the personal family circle, the elementary teacher cannot avoid influencing the impressionable child in ways beyond the formal curriculum. We can illustrate this in two areas of politically relevant learning: obedience and competitiveness.

In a French village school, four- and five-year-olds are started in the *classes enfantines.* A teacher responsible for these young charges reports: "There is nothing serious that they have to learn for a year or so." Laurence Wylie, studying the village school, thinks differently: "The four-year-old and five-year-old children, however, *do* learn important lessons.

They learn to sit still for long periods. They learn to accept the discipline of the school. . . . They are not encouraged to 'express their personality.' On the contrary they learn that their personality must be kept constantly under control." [25] Wylie's observation probably applies to most school systems. The lesson of obedience is learned early and is very important for political and social life.

Evidence from American elementary school children links the "lesson of obedience" more closely with political learning. Elementary teachers place more emphasis on compliance to rules and authority than any other "political" topic. Second- and third-grade teachers consider the obligation of the child to conform to school rules and laws of the community a more important lesson than reading and arithmetic. This concern with compliance appears to be characteristic of teachers of all elementary grades.[26] Although teachers emphasize compliance, they underemphasize the right of citizens to participate in government. Hess and Torney conclude that "much of what is called citizenship training in the public schools does not teach the child about the city, state, or national government, but is an attempt to teach regard for the rules and standards of conduct of the school." [27] There are critics of American schools who feel that the emphasis on obedience damages children. This damage makes it very difficult for them to play meaningful roles in an open, democratic polity. Writes one such critic:

> Far from helping students to develop into mature, self-reliant, self-motivated individuals, schools seem to do everything they can to keep youngsters in a state of chronic, almost infantile, dependency. The pervasive atmosphere of distrust, together with rules covering the most minute aspects of existence, teach students every day that they are not people of worth, and certainly not individuals capable of regulating their own behavior.[28]

25 Wylie, *op. cit.,* p. 57.
26 Hess and Torney, *op. cit.,* p. 110.
27 *Ibid.,* p. 218.
28 Charles E. Silberman, *Crisis in the Classroom* (New York: Random House, 1970), p. 134.

Competitiveness is another politically meaningful orientation learned in the classroom. The authors of a leading textbook on education in the United States write: "The child learns that it is serious to fail, important to succeed, that the society disapproves of slow people and rewards fast ones." [29] A simple fourth-grade spelling contest conveys this lesson. Whether or not the student masters the intricacies of spelling, he or she internalizes the cultural value of competitiveness and success.

A comparison of the "lesson in competitiveness" learned by the American fourth-grader with that taught to the Israeli fourth-grader in the kibbutz is instructive. The philosophy of kibbutz education is to minimize competition among students. Students are not graded. No competitive rating system is used to reward or punish. Students cannot fail; all are promoted at the end of the year. The cultural value of equality, it is thought, would be compromised if schools rewarded performance differentially.[30] The kibbutz pattern is interesting primarily as a deviation. Most schools attempt to elicit performance by comparing one student with another.

In an article, "The School Class as a Social System," Talcott Parsons enlarges on the notion of the learning culture as a socialization experience.[31] He points out that the child enters school with only one social role clearly determined, that of being a boy or a girl. Beyond that, the child is free to choose among the available roles. He or she can be a worker or a player, a leader or a follower, well behaved or a problem child, a success or a failure, and so on. A boy's status as the son in his family is fixed by his biological characteristics; his status in the classroom social system will be fixed by how he performs valued tasks. His status is achieved rather than ascribed. In this regard the classroom as a social system reflects the larger social and political systems more than does the family. At least in American society, the expectation is that a

[29] Robert J. Havighurst and Bernice L. Neugarten, *Society and Education* (Boston: Allyn & Bacon, 1957), p. 508.

[30] For an extended discussion of this point see Spiro, *op. cit.*, pp. 258–264.

[31] Talcott Parsons, "The School Class as a Social System," *Harvard Educational Review*, XXIV (1959), pp. 297–318.

person gets what he deserves. His rights are an equal chance and the rewards of his efforts. In Parson's words, "There is thus a basic sense in which the elementary school class is an embodiment of the fundamental American value of equality of opportunity, in that it places value *both* on initial equality and on differential achievement." [32]

The basic point here is that attitudes toward achievement, toward change, toward fair play, toward manipulability of the environment, toward cooperation, as well as toward obedience and competitiveness, can be shaped by the cultures of the classroom. Such components of one's world have important "spillover" effects and shape political outlooks.

The amount of harmony between the values shaped in the classroom and those applicable to the political world do vary, of course. In East Africa there is today considerable discrepancy between the school culture and the national ideology. Although the political leaders stress egalitarian democracy, the schools are run by an elitist, hierarchic prefectorial system. Although the political leaders stress African socialism, the classrooms remain wedded to the norm of individual achievement. The values implicitly transmitted by the school as a social system are incongruent with the articulated national aspirations. [33]

A similar lack of harmony has been noted in connection with American schooling. There is on the one hand an emphasis on democratic values, yet on the other hand an emphasis on efficiency and control by school authorities. The student is faced with numerous, seemingly petty regulations concerning dress, movement in the halls, silence, codes of conduct, and so forth. The implications for democratic citizenship are bleak, according to many writers.

> For some years now, it has been clear that the American educational system is not the bastion of democracy it is labeled in the national ideology. Values and the cultural myths of equality and opportunity are memorized, and the mundane problems

[32] *Ibid.,* p. 309.
[33] See Kenneth Prewitt (ed.), *Education and Political Values: Essays about East Africa* (Nairobi: East African Publishing House, 1969), pp. 18–19.

of a representative system are analyzed. Elections and voting are even walked through. Everywhere the power of the flag and the President's picture shelter the school symbolically, and the stigmata of democracy are ritualistically displayed. Yet the political and social structure of our schools is not democratic, and many graduates of these socializing institutions are emerging class-conscious and difference-conscious, with an abiding lack of faith in the capability of their fellows to govern either themselves or their country.[34]

Another writer, summarizing his study of nearly 7,000 high school students, reports that a "large majority of the students feel they are regularly subjected to undemocratic decisions. These are seen as unilateral actions by teachers and administrators that deny fundamental rights of persons to equality, dissent or due process, and of some members of an institution to some meaningful share in its rule-making processes." [35]

Such findings and assertions should be treated cautiously. A great deal of additional evidence would have to be collected before concluding that the American schools systematically inhibit the acquisition of democratic values. Critics notwithstanding, it is evident that millions of high school graduates do participate actively in democratic politics when they reach adulthood. They vote, join political groups, discuss politics, and express commitment to democratic values and procedures. The evidence, then, suggests a mixed picture. Although it is true that obedience, conformity, and compliance are stressed in public schools, so are other values — such as initiative, independent thinking, questioning, and curiosity.

What is suggested by the critics is the importance of paying some attention to the role of teachers as models of authoritarian versus democratic values. Teachers can stress disciplined learning of the material presented, rigid adherence to rules, and a deferential attitude toward themselves as the authority. Student participation may be kept to a minimum. Or, teachers may assume an opposite stance. More student

[34] Elizabeth Leonie Simpson, *Democracy's Stepchildren* (San Francisco: Jossey-Bass, 1971), p. 2.

[35] Allen Weston and Dean Murphy, "Civic Education in a Crisis Age: An Alternative to Revolution and Repression" (Mimeographed, September 1970), pp. 2–3.

participation may be encouraged. School rules may be few and relaxed. Teachers may require less deference from students.

The crucial notion for political socialization is that these conditions might affect the political outlook of the students. Democratic leadership by the teacher fosters attitudes and skills consonant with democratic values. The authoritarian teacher induces his or her charges to think according to hierarchy and deference to power. This notion has two variants: One line of reasoning stresses the teacher as a role model, the other concerns the importance of student participation for learning.

Postwar Germany provides an interesting example of the application of this proposition about classroom atmosphere. Both the occupation forces after the war and the new German government were concerned with remaking Germany into a democracy. Education was to be the key to this transformation. Curriculum reform was considered only a part of the effort needed. Attention was focused also on the method of instruction and the social atmosphere of the schools. "The classroom was to be more democratic, and student participation in the administration of school was to be fostered." [36] It is too early to evaluate the success of this program, but it is interesting that 38 percent of German students who were age twelve between 1946 and 1953, and only 6 percent who were age twelve between 1941 and 1945 reported actual participation in school discussions and debates.[37] These data suggest that alterations in the classroom atmosphere are possible. Whether such alterations can have the desired political effect cannot yet be ascertained.

SUMMARY

We have now reviewed three ways in which the formal classroom and educational program serve as political socialization agents: the curriculum, the ritual life, and the teacher. It

[36] Sidney Verba, "Germany: The Remaking of Political Culture," in Lucian Pye and Sidney Verba (eds.), *Political Culture and Political Development* (Princeton: Princeton University Press, 1965), p. 161.

[37] These data are computed from a table presented in Gabriel Almond and Sidney Verba, *The Civic Culture* (Princeton: Princeton University Press, 1963), p. 339.

should be quite apparent that the school molds political characteristics in both direct and indirect ways. The classroom in a number of different ways serves as an agent of political learning, one that is often employed consciously and deliberately by society's leaders to insure political support and knowledge. We now turn to some of the less formal aspects that affect the process of political maturation.

NONCLASSROOM FORMS
THE SOCIAL COMPOSITION OF THE SCHOOL

Educational theorists and cultural engineers have long sought to use the social composition of schools for the specific purposes of influencing political orientations. The social class, ethnic, racial, tribal, and religious makeup of the student and staff population of a school are assumed to influence the views students have toward social groupings in society at large. In the United States, the mass public school system has long been accepted and promoted as a contributor to intergroup equality and cooperation. The traditional, class-based schools of Britain, on the other hand, have contributed to a more socially stratified culture and a system in which leadership has been drawn largely from the upper classes.

The current controversy in American cities over bussing students from diversified areas of a city to mixed schools in order to insure racial and socially integrated classrooms illustrates well the importance placed on the social composition of the schools. Both opponents and proponents of bussing base their argument on the premise that the composition of the student body has consequences for social and political learning. The proponents argue that students from various social class and racial backgrounds should be brought together in common facilities to counteract residential segregation, to promote multigroup understanding, and to avoid teaching racial discrimination. An argument advanced by opponents of bussing is that neighborhood schools should be preserved to maintain neighborhood identification, activity, and cooperation. Each neighborhood should have its own exclusive school with which it identifies.

Although the goals of these positions are at odds, they share a common socialization proposition. A person's contacts with other individuals affect his or her way of viewing the social and political world. The composition of a student body can aid in the development of community identification or prevent it. It can help create intergroup cooperation and harmony, or isolation and conflict. Of the many social institutions the child knows, the school is most important in this regard. The school is the first major institution most children have experience with outside the limited and protective shell of the family. When the child enters the formal educational system, he or she is confronted with a larger and more diversified population of peers and authority figures than he or she experienced in the home or in the smaller, neighborhood peer groups. From these new contacts the young child learns about articulating and solving collective problems, about asserting and protecting rights in competition with others, and about the possibilities of social cooperation or conflict.

Whether the school population is socially homogeneous or whether it more accurately reflects the heterogeneity of the adult world will affect social adjustment patterns. In particular, the child's development of stereotypes and prejudices is influenced by the makeup of the school population. In Chapter III we pointed out that a basic component of the political self is a set of social categories, identifications, and prejudices through which to filter political happenings. The development of these filters is significantly influenced by the social composition of this first major nonfamily group. In many instances the school, which tries to promote social integration and toleration through a socially diversified student body, is working directly against the socialization of the more particularistic family. Family training is often geared toward a more exclusive social outlook, toward differentiating family members from other groups of people.

Most of the specific attention to social composition has been directed toward its effect upon prejudice and discrimination. Contact with diversified types of people is assumed to facilitate understanding and cooperation between groups. Studies of the actual results of such integration have yielded mixed findings. On balance, however, most observers feel that increased contact between various groupings in society aids in the creation of a political order in which cooperation among groups replaces patterns of discrimination and hostility. A segregated society and a segregated school system heighten the tendency toward rigid and inaccurate stereotyping. As one student of race relations has put it: "Prejudices are generally acquired slowly and over a period of time. The child acquires his ethnic values and racial attitudes as he learns other social lessons from adults, from his peers, and from his life experiences. Groups that are segregated in schools or in the community he assumes are inferior because society treats them as inferiors." [38] This was recognized in the famous 1954 Supreme Court decision on public school segregation. The Court held that the maintenance of segregated schools institutionalized cultural patterns of prejudice, and caused whites and blacks to share a set of values contributing to barriers between them.

We have emphasized the manipulation of the school composition as a means of increasing cooperation and understanding. Of course, many societies compose their schools for the opposite reason. In some instances, as in South Africa, this is the intention of a national educational plan. More often, however, group differentiation is promoted by special subgroup schools. Numerous subgroups in society (racial, religious, ethnic, and social class) seek to promote group values and to differentiate themselves specifically from the rest of society. They establish their own school systems primarily to keep their members from close contact with other groups in the society. By limiting the social diversity of their schools and keeping their children out of more socially integrated public schools, particular in-group feelings and parochial loyalties can be promoted. The basic goal in this instance is different from the general goal of social integration, but the same major socialization variable is at work.

[38] M. Vosk, "Correlates of Prejudice," *Review of Educational Research,* XXIII (1953), pp. 353–361. Quoted in Bernard Berelson and Gary A. Steiner, *Human Behavior* (New York: Harcourt, Brace & World, 1964), p. 507.

EXTRACURRICULAR ACTIVITIES AND STUDENT
POLITICAL GROUPS

In addition to their formal academic programs most schools maintain extracurricular activities and groups. The number of such activities varies greatly from culture to culture. Their proliferation is extensive in the United States, where the academic program of the average school is supplemented by dozens of clubs, performing groups, student governments, and athletic activities.

We can distinguish between two forms of groups. There are first, numerous groups concerned with school affairs or occupational preparation, for example, student government, music and dramatic groups, and sports. In addition, many schools have, either officially or unofficially, connections with specifically political organizations. In some instances, such as the Young Pioneers in the Soviet Union and the Hitler Youth in Nazi Germany, they are regulated and sponsored by the government. In others they are sponsored by political parties or other partisan groups. In the United States branches of the Young Republicans and Young Democrats, public action groups, and various civil rights and peace groups are more specifically political organizations. Both types of organization have consequences for citizenship and political training, but their influence is different.

School-Based Activities. Those activities specifically tied in with the school are thought by some to train the student for political participation and teach him or her the cultural values associated with it. At least extracurricular activities have been promoted by school officials for just these reasons. One observer comments on their utility as follows:

> The extracurricular activity was given an important position in the philosophy of the democratic school. High school extracurricular activities were to be analogous to adult voluntary associations. Just as a membership in a voluntary association was believed to have positive effects on an adult's citizenship competence, so would the extracurricular activity have positive

effects on the teenager. Participation would give him insight and awareness into social processes. He would acquire an ability to manipulate these processes. He would have a greater understanding of how things get done in the larger political system. He would have a more positive orientation toward political phenomena. So the argument went.[39]

The possible consequences of these activities are varied. The sports programs of the schools may teach the student the culturally prescribed values of competition and sportsmanship. In American society the student is taught to compete, to seek to win, but to do so within the proper "rules of the game." He or she is also taught to lose with good grace. Such norms are, of course, generally appropriate for broad aspects of adult social life. In other cultures the appropriate values of the society are also learned through the procedures surrounding various sports.

Student governments are set up, by and large, to teach the student the values of self-government and to familiarize him or her with the forms and procedures he or she will face in the adult political world. For a minority of students, student governments provide direct experiences in governmental positions, which are generally designed in form and title as prototypes of the governmental institutions of the adult political world.

As with other aspects of school life, it is difficult to assess the effect of extracurricular activities. Research on these relationships is sparse, and contradictory. There are at least three different arguments to be found in the research literature: the argument that extracurricular activities have a positive influence on political attitudes; that is, students active in such extracurricular clubs and programs develop a greater appreciation of actual political institutions and expect to be politically active in adult life.[40] A contrary argument is that there is no carryover from extracurricular activity to political

---

[39] David Ziblatt, "High School Extracurricular Activities and Political Socialization," in *The Annals of the American Academy of Political and Social Science,* CCCLXI (September 1965), p. 23.

[40] Helen Sonnenburg Lewis, "The Teen-age Joiner and his Orientation Toward Public Affairs: A Test of Two Multiple Group Membership Hypotheses" (Ph.D. dissertation, Department of Political Science, Michigan State University, 1962), quoted in Ziblatt, *ibid.,* p. 24.

views and adult participation. However political its form, the content of high school club activities is social; and such social activities really have no bearing on adult political life.[41] The third argument was introduced earlier. Critics believe that the "democratic student government" is really a sham, and that students recognize it for the sham it is and actually carry away from such experiences a feeling of political futility. None of these arguments has received the research attention that would warrant definitive conclusions.

Student Political Groups and Activities: A minority of students get involved in student political organizations as part of their school experiences. Such experiences strongly affect the political learning of those involved. Through his or her involvement in political demonstrations, movements, and organizations the student comes into direct contact with the political world. As one commentator has put it, student organizations concerned with politics "are usually the main source of political education for the students involved in them, and often have a vital and lasting effect on those involved." [42]

The amount of political participation and involvement in student political organizations varies from nation to nation, but nowhere does it involve more than a small minority of the student body. The popular picture of a whole student body participating in riots and demonstrations is a distorted one for the college and university populations of the developing countries, as well as for those of more developed nations.[43] S. M. Lipset estimates that the combined membership of the junior affiliates of United States political parties constitute about 2 percent of the total student population.[44]

[41] Ziblatt, *op. cit.*, p. 31. See also Richard M. Merelman, *Political Socialization and Educational Climates* (New York: Holt, Rinehart and Winston, 1971), p. 141.

[42] Philip G. Altbach, "Students and Politics," *Comparative Education Review*, X (1966), p. 185. This issue of the *Comparative Education Review*, edited by S. M. Lipset, is devoted to student politics. Many of the ideas of this section are drawn from this volume.

[43] Claucio A. D. Soares, "The Active Few: Student Ideology and Participation in Developing Countries," *ibid.*, p. 205.

[44] Quoted in S. M. Lipset and Philip G. Altbach, "Student Politics and Higher Education in the United States," *ibid.*, p. 320.

The amount, form, and direction of student participation in politics differs greatly from nation to nation, and from one generation to another. In Latin American countries university students have traditionally been forces in national politics, and students are politically active in greater proportions than are students in North America. Asian and African students have played critical roles in their independence movements and continue to play active parts in national politics. Some generations of students seem more prone to political involvement than others. In the United States the 1930s was a period of student interest and participation. The late 1940s and 1950s are generally regarded as a period of student political apathy. The 1960s witnessed a period of renewed political interest; students participated in the Civil Rights movement, the peace movement, in programs designed to help underprivileged elements of the population, and in attempts to democratize the schools. In other nations other factors have been the cause of student political involvement. In France the war years and involvement in the resistance continue to influence contemporary student politics. Colonial control gave rise to student demonstrations in India, Algeria, and numerous other colonial areas after World War II and up through the mid-1960s. Disaffection with national policies and administrations have mobilized student activists in Thailand, Korea, South Vietnam, Spain, and the Sudan.

The forms, causes, and results of student political participation form a complex picture. There seem to be at least a few general patterns, however. First, student political involvement tends to radicalize political orientations. Whatever political views a student has, leftist or rightist, they tend to be intensified and radicalized in the crucible of student politics. Several factors account for this. The student is "acting out" his political views in a highly emotional situation, as part of a collective that gives him support and feeds his political commitments. The student frequently feels shut out of normal avenues of political expression. He or she is too young to vote and often ignored by elders. He or she generally has fewer direct responsibilities in society and thus has fewer restraints.

Second, although both right- and left-oriented students are

radicalized through involvement, students of liberal orientations are more likely to become engaged in student movements than are their conservative classmates. This bias results from the fact that left-leaning students tend more than rightists to view studenthood as part of, rather than preliminary to, an adult citizen role. It also stems from the general tendency for colleges to be more congenial to liberally oriented student groups than to conservative ones.

Third, although only a small minority of the student population are activists, student movements influence a much larger part of the student population. Nonactivist sympathizers as well as student onlookers find themselves altering political views in accord with the opinion leadership provided by the activists. The activists often define or redefine political issues in such a way that all segments of the student body will respond and thus reformulate political outlooks.

For a small number of participants, political groups serve as recruiting agencies for adult political roles. Many political organizations sponsor student groups as a means of finding future leaders for their own organizations. Likewise some students, already set on political careers, use student political groups as stepping stones for adult political aspirations. In either case student political organizations are probably important sources of experience, for future political leaders and participants.

EDUCATION AND POLITICAL ORIENTATIONS

In this section we discuss the actual status of being educated as it affects political orientations. Numerous surveys demonstrate that well-educated persons differ politically from less well-educated persons in many important respects. Level of education, either as an indicator of other social characteristics or as an attribute in its own right, is universally correlated with many aspects of the political self.

V. O. Key has summarized American research findings bearing on how education affects political outlooks: (a) Better educated persons feel a stronger sense of duty to participate in the political life of the nation than do less well-educated persons. (b) The educated citizen is more apt to feel that he or she can influence the political process, that governmental officials have regard for him and his views, and that channels of access to political power are open to him. (c) The better educated the citizen is, the more interested and involved he or she will be in political matters. (d) Finally, education is strongly related to political activity. The better educated vote at a greater rate. They are also likely to engage in more demanding types of political participation such as campaigning, working for a political party, and contributing money.[45]

Cross-national studies have reported similar findings. Almond and Verba, for instance, note nine major ways in which the educated in the five nations they studied differ substantially from the less well-educated: [46]

1. The more educated person is more aware of the impact of government on the individual than is the person of less education.

2. The more educated individual is more likely to report that he follows politics and pays attention to election campaigns than is the individual of less education.

3. The more educated individual has more political information.

4. The more educated individual has opinions on a wider range of political subjects; the focus of his attention to politics is wider.

5. The more educated individual is more likely to engage in political discussion.

6. The more educated individual feels free to discuss politics with a wider range of people. Those with less education are more likely to report that there are many people with whom they avoid such discussions.

7. The more educated individual is more likely to consider himself capable of influencing the government; that is reflected both in responses to questions on what one could do about an unjust law and in respondent's scores on the subjective competence scale.

8. The more educated individual is more likely to be a member — an active member — of some organizations.

45 Key, *op. cit.*, pp. 323–331.
46 Almond and Verba, *op. cit.*, pp. 380–381.

9. The more educated individual is more likely to express confidence in his social environment: to believe that other people are trustworthy and helpful.

There is little question that the level of education affects a citizens' perception of the political world and his or her relationships with it. This form of influence operates in addition to the more direct effect of the schools as agents of political learning. In the bulk of this chapter we have considered how the schools provide the student with direct political education and with experiences that have latent consequences for political orientations. Here we are suggesting that "being educated" itself affects such matters as political knowledge, involvement, and sense of political ability and efficacy.

The factors causing this strong relationship between level of education and key political orientations are many and complex. We can offer four explanatory hypotheses as an initial step in explaining the relationships. An additional word of caution is needed before we proceed, however. One difficulty in assessing the influence of education on political attitudes, is that the level of education is closely related to a number of other socioeconomic attributes — especially to income, occupation, and social class. These other factors are strongly related to political orientations. For that reason it is difficult to isolate the independent effect of education. In the points that follow we make no pretense at successful control of these other factors.

1. Better educated persons are involved in society's communication network. Their reading habits, travel experiences, friendship patterns, and leisure activities increase the amount of politically pertinent information available to them. Education is a skill that helps a person to act out this information, as well.

2. Citizens of higher educational status are accustomed to collective decision making. The educated are active participants in the organizational life of society. Through his social involvement, the educated person acquires habits and skills that are easily transferred to political affairs.

3. The educated citizen also acquires attitudes that are

transferred to the political sphere. A clear illustration of this is the feeling of political competence. The educated tend to believe that rational manipulation of social institutions can produce desired goals. This sense of mastery and control over the social environment is generalized to politics, and the educated feel more politically efficacious than the uneducated.

4. Educated persons, because of their higher social and economic status, usually feel a greater stake in society. More than the uneducated, they presume that political events directly affect their personal well-being. The more active role taken in politics by the better educated stems, in part, from a desire to protect their investments.

This attempt to account for the relationship between level of education and participation in politics suggests an observation about general political socialization theory. Although certain basic aspects of the political self are established prior to adulthood, political learning continues beyond childhood and adolescence. The citizen's style of actual political participation is not firmly established by preadult socialization. It is during the adult years that opportunities become available for engagement in political activities. In this section we have reviewed how it is that tendencies toward active political involvement are linked to the resources and experiences available to the better educated in society. Particular political socialization experiences, therefore, are distributed in society according to social status.

THE SCHOOLS AND POLITICAL SOCIALIZATION

In most societies the school stands with the family and peer groups as one of the most significant agents of political learning. Under some conditions its influence is likely to be even greater than these other two socialization agents. Like the family, the school influences the child and adolescent during the crucial formative years. The school provides the adolescent citizen with knowledge about the political world and his or her role in it. It equips the child with more concrete perceptions of political institutions and relationships. The school also transmits the consensual values and attitudes of the society. Except in the case of special subgroup schools and youth organizations affiliated with political parties, the school has little direct effect on the development of partisan values or subgroup loyalties.

In contrast to the family and peer groups, schools are susceptible to centralized and uniform control. One of the key attributes of the family and peer groups as sources of political orientations, as we have said, is their tendency to be decentralized, nondeliberate, and haphazard. Schools, of course, operate differently. It is possible for a given regime to design, and in some instances to implement, a fairly uniform program of political education and indoctrination for the vast majority of the children and adolescents of an entire society. Common political values and information can be disseminated in a fairly uniform way to a large proportion of a nation's young people. Political socialization in the schools is often more deliberate than that of the family and peer groups. Most political regimes and educational administrators accept citizenship training and political indoctrination as an important part of education.

Although political education programs are more uniform, manipulable, and deliberate than the family and peer group teaching, they generally fall short of total control and uniform effect. Uniformity of program and intention seldom means uniformity of application. Even the most centralized school system has trouble manipulating all the politically relevant messages communicated in all of its classrooms. Even when there is uniformity of intention, different teachers and different classrooms are not equally effective. As we pointed out before, students differ in their receptiveness to political messages communicated in the classroom.

Despite the many factors working against uniform political socialization in the schools, schools remain one of the more controllable sources of political learning. A society seeking to bring about large-scale and rapid changes in political values will find the educational system among the most effective means for implementing uniform alterations. The leaders of totalitarian nations and of the new nations generally have accepted this and have expended resources in the development of schools and political education programs in them.

Indeed, in no nation have political leaders ignored the socialization consequences of the schools. In an otherwise routine speech about the virtues of America's free enterprise system, William E. Simon, then secretary of the Treasury, instructed his audience of businessmen and public relations experts as follows:

> I would advise, however, that you counsel your bosses and your clients to take a close look at the teaching policies of those schools and foundations being considered for corporate gifts. Find out if the subjects of that generosity are really assisting in the fight to maintain our freedoms or if they are working to erode them — and urge that judgments be made accordingly.[47]

In short, this influential national leader was telling the business community to provide financial support to schools that taught the economic and political values Simon presumably shared with his audience, but financially to squeeze those schools less orthodox in their teaching.

The *New York Times,* one of the leading liberal newspapers in the United States, editorially criticized Simon for his "shocking lack of understanding of academic freedom." It is a pity, the *Times* wrote, "that Mr. Simon, who is so protective of the freedom of the business community, would incite that community to restrict or censor the freedom of education." [48]

We need not take sides in this argument to see the implications of political socialization in any nation's educational system. What is taught, who teaches it, to whom, and under what circumstances will never be free of political and economic pressures. The stakes are simply too high for those in control not to attempt to influence who learns what, especially as that learning affects basic political values.

[47] Quoted in a *New York Times* editorial titled "Eroding School Freedom," March 7, 1976.
[48] *Ibid.*

CHAPTER IX

Social Groups and Political Learning

THE SOCIAL CONTEXT OF POLITICAL OUTLOOKS

Any close observer of political attitudes and behavior is likely to discover some significant patterning of political preferences and behavior. If he takes note of party preferences and voting choices among a large number of people, he is likely to observe that people from the same racial and ethnic backgrounds, as well as those in the same income and occupational categories, tend to have similar partisan preferences. If he discusses political issues with several people who have known each other for a long period, he may be struck by the similarity in viewpoints expressed by the close friends. If he is a member of an occupational organization, such as a labor union or professional group, of a religious or civic organization, or of a fraternal or sports association, he is likely to find that from time to time these organizations take positions on political issues of special concern to them. He may also have felt pressure from the group to support the stand it takes.

Such an observer, if he were inclined to make generalizations, might be led to affirm one of the most significant facts of political and social life. The attitudes and values of people tend to be formed, sustained, and altered by the group and associational ties of which they are a part. The family and the school are not the only associations that influence political thinking and preferences. A wide variety of groups help to shape political orientations.[1] In this chapter we discuss the impact of various types of social groups upon political learning. In considering group impact we make distinctions among three different group forms and show how and why each type influences the content, strength, and stability of political orientations.

As close observers of social and political life, sociologists, social psychologists, and political scientists have noted that individual outlooks and behavior tend to be related to social position and to group ties. The group context of attitudes and behavior has been one of the most extensively investigated and documented areas in the study of social behavior.[2] The fact of group influence has been noted in political orientations as well as for other outlooks. Three different types of evidence point to the important influence of groups in political life.

First, numerous studies of political attitudes and behavior have found relationships between political predispositions and the position of people in various social and economic groupings.[3] People who share common economic or occupational positions often are found to vote alike and to take similar positions on political issues. For example, since the Great Depression of the 1930s working-class people in the United States have tended to vote for candidates of the Democratic party. Members of the same religious, ethnic, and racial groupings often look at the political world in ways similar to each other, and different from those in other groupings. Blacks in contemporary American society tend to be overwhelmingly liberal on social and economic issues. On many such issues whites are concentrated more on the conservative side.[4] In some instances political outlooks are associated with differences in age, sex, or geographic area.

Second, studies of opinions and political preferences have found that individuals tend to share common opinions with

---

[1] The family and the school can be considered groups. However, because of their particularly significant roles in political socialization they were considered separately in the two preceding chapters.

[2] This issue is discussed in S. M. Lipset, *Political Man* (New York: Doubleday, 1960), especially chs. 6 to 8.

[3] *Ibid.*

[4] See Richard E. Dawson, *Public Opinion and Contemporary Disarray* (New York: Harper and Row, 1973), pp. 116–124.

those people with whom they spend a lot of time and have close relationships. Husbands and wives, close friends, and work associates tend to look at the political and social world in similar ways.[5] Similar outlooks are also commonly found among members of the same groups or organizations.

Third, studies and experiments with small groups have analyzed how individual opinions, values, and even perceptions of physical objects are influenced by the positions taken by others in the same group. There is a tendency for one to adopt the opinion held by most of the members of the group or to alter one's opinion so it corresponds more closely with that of other group members. Small group studies have not only shown that opinions among group associates tend to be similar, they have analyzed how and why small groups exercise so much impact on norms and behavior.[6]

In analyzing how and why political learning is affected by social groups it is important to distinguish between three different group forms. The three forms are: (1) societal groupings, (2) primary groups, and (3) secondary groups. These three types of groups entail different relationships among members or identifiers. Each has considerable impact on political socialization. However, they exert that influence in different ways. Too often, discussions of group influence do not distinguish among these different group forms. Associations as diverse as economic classes, close-knit friendship cliques, and labor union locals are often discussed as if they were essentially the same thing. A clear picture of group influence and a better understanding of how each affects political learning is enhanced by drawing distinctions and noting the different ways in which they affect political learning.

SOCIETAL GROUPINGS AND POLITICAL OUTLOOKS

We use the term *societal groupings* to refer to the broad categories of individuals who are tied together by some particular characteristics and common identities. Societies are

---

[5] See, Angus Campbell, Gerald Gurin, and Warren E. Miller. *The Voter Decides* (New York: Harper & Row, 1954), pp. 199–206.

[6] See, for example, Dorwin Cartwright and Alvin Zander, *Group Dynamics: Research and Theory* (New York: Harper, 1960); and Sidney Verba, *Small Groups and Political Behavior* (Princeton, N.J.: Princeton University Press, 1961).

composed of a number of socially significant categories. These include collectivities such as social classes, occupations, races, religious identifiers, geographic regions, and age cohorts. Individuals are part of these broad groupings because they share certain characteristics. These can be physical attributes as is the case with race and sex groupings. They can be shared beliefs or values as in the case of religious and ethnic groupings. They can entail holding similar positions in social or occupational strata as is the case with economic classes and occupational groupings. They can also be based on geographic location. Societal groupings can vary greatly in size. Regional groupings and economic classes can involve a large segment of the total population. Others such as particular religious, ethnic, and racial groupings may constitute only small minorities.

We use the term societal grouping here to underscore the point that these categories should be distinguished from other types of groups. By any strict definition they are not "groups." They lack the structure and processes of interaction that characterize secondary groups. Their "members" do not have the close personalized ties that are so important in primary groups. A societal grouping such as the working class and American blacks should be differentiated from a labor union and the NAACP. The latter groups may draw their members from the working class and blacks, respectively. They may presume to serve as spokespieces for those collectivities, but they are different phenomena. These distinctions are important in understanding how and why individuals are influenced by social groups. Societal groupings do not act as agents of socialization in the same way that primary and secondary groups do. Close friends can communicate their political positions to each other and in this way influence each other's political outlooks. A labor union local and a branch of the NAACP can adopt an official position on political issues and make an effort to get their members and identifiers to accept that position. The working class, senior citizens, and blacks as large collectivities are not in a position to take stands and to educate and/or pressure their identifiers to follow those positions; although we sometimes think and speak as if they do.

Societal groupings, nonetheless, can have a tremendous influence on political perspectives. Study after study of party preferences, policy choices, level of political participation, and ideological position have shown that persons in different economic classes, occupations, races, ethnic or religious groupings, and so on tend to hold different political viewpoints.

Most studies dealing with the relationships between societal groupings and political life have looked at adults. There is some evidence to suggest that political differences between individuals in different groupings may begin to form quite early. Partisan attachments, as we suggested earlier, are not only formed early in life, they tend to be related to the family ties with various class, ethnic, racial, and religious groupings. Robert Hess and Judith Torney find that some political perspectives are already related to class background in the elementary school years: [7]

> . . . lower status children more frequently accept authority figures as right and rely on their trustworthiness and benign intent. There is, therefore, more acquiescence to the formal structure and less tendency to question the motivations behind the behavior of government and governmental officials.

They also found that higher status children have higher levels of interest and a greater sense of efficacy in the political world. Social status background is related to party preferences beginning by about grade 5, and becomes increasingly pronounced in successively higher grades.

The existence of relationships between what we call societal categories and political life is so well documented that there is no need to discuss it in detail here. The central issue for us is how these relationships fit into the socialization process. How do these social and economic groupings come to structure political life? We have already pointed out that societal groupings do not serve as agents of socialization in the way other types of groups do. How, then, do they affect political orientations? We suggest that they influence political life in two important ways. First, they serve as important reference or identification points. Second, they tend to structure the

[7] Robert D. Hess and Judith V. Torney, *The Development of Political Attitudes in Children* (Chicago: Aldine, 1967), pp. 126–127.

relationships individuals have with other groups and associations that can serve as agents of socialization.

People become part of various societal groupings on the basis of having particular characteristics and by identifying themselves as part of the particular grouping. Being part of a class or a race or an ethnic group takes on particular meaning to individuals because they come to identify with that group. They form an attachment to it and see themselves as part of it. On the basis of these identifications societal groupings tend to serve as reference points or conceptual filters for the individual's perceptions of the political world. The individual forms an attachment with a particular societal grouping, and that identification affects the way he or she sees the world. Racial identification, social-class identity, and other such attachments in this sense become part of the political self. They are part of the basic self-identification of the individual, and part of the self-interpretation through which he or she understands and evaluates the world of politics.

The Jew, for example, identifies himself as Jewish. He sees himself as part of the Jewish people and being part of the Jewish people is one of the ways he understands who he is. As he becomes aware of the political world and understands his particular place in it, that Jewish identification serves as an important reference point for relating to the political world. He may make political evaluations and choices on the basis of this Jewish perspective.[8] What is the Jewish position on a particular political issue? What party or candidate is going to be best for the interests of the Jews?

Numerous other social categories or societal groupings operate in the same way. The Catholic may make political choices on the basis of the teaching of the Church on a particular issue. The working-class identifier may decide to vote according to which candidate will best represent the interests of the working man. Old people may try to find the candidate who is most sensitive to the plight of the aged. The crucial

[8] For a discussion of the political behavior of American Jews, see Lawrence H. Fuchs, *The Political Behavior of American Jews* (New York: The Free Press, 1956).

means through which societal groupings affect political learning and outlooks is by serving as important political reference points.

Identifications and attachments with these societal groupings affect political learning in another way as well. They play a role in structuring social contacts and thus exposure to socialization influences. The individual's position in social groupings determines, in large measure, what types of political learning experiences he or she will have. The tendency of members of common group attachments to live, work, and socialize with each other restricts exposure to diverse socialization influences. There are working-class neighborhoods, middle-class neighborhoods, black neighborhoods, Jewish neighborhoods, and a vast array of other ethnic and class-identified neighborhoods. Because people in a particular social category tend to make friends, marry, and associate with "their own kind," the political and social views they are exposed to tend to be homogeneous, and also to reflect the particular outlooks of the societal groupings to which they are attached.

Two other points about the impact of societal groupings on political outlooks need to be touched on here: (1) the early acquisition of group attachments, and (2) the shifting political relevance of attachments to societal groupings.

In Chapter IV we pointed out that attachments or identifications with societal groupings are among the earliest social orientations acquired by the child. Attachments with class, race, religious, and regional groupings are often formed by the preschool years. They are acquired by the individual at the same point he or she is picking up basic national identification and attachments to political symbols and authorities. We suggested then that possibly one of the reasons these various attachments to societal groupings become so significant politically is that they are often formed in conjunction with basic political attachments. The fact that the young American learns to be an American, a Catholic, and a Democrat all about the same time helps to explain both the persistence and close relationship of these identifications. Being a Catholic and a Democrat and an American all become intertwined in the individual's self-perception.

Identification with various societal groupings becomes politically important because such identifications can serve as important political reference points.[9] The political relevance of various societal groupings will not necessarily remain constant. At one point in time one type of social grouping may loom very large in shaping and structuring political outlooks. At another point that grouping may become less important and other groups rise in significance. During most of the period since the Civil War regional identifications have been significant as a reference point. The significance of regional identification was particularly important for southerners. Southerners tended to see their relationship to the national government and to political parties as somewhat different from that of people in other regions. In the last two decades regional identification has decreased in political relevance.[10] During the 1930s, the years of the Great Depression and the coming of the New Deal, social-class identification emerged as an important political reference grouping. Salient political issues tended to be class relevant. Party identification and voting preferences tended to follow class lines. During the late 1960s class identification became less important as a reference point.[11] The salient issues of the period, for example, race relations, Vietnam, and public order, were not peculiarly class related. One could speak of the "working-class position" and the "business position" on issues such as fair labor standards and government regulation of business, the types of policy issues that were highly salient in the 1930s and 1940s. However, it was difficult to identify a particular working-class position on Vietnam or the business position on school integration. On the other hand, racial identification has become an important political reference point on a number of contemporary issues.[12] During the late 1960s the widespread reference to the

9 This notion is close to the use of the concept reference group or to what V. O. Key broadened to the concept reference symbol. See V. O. Key, Jr., *Public Opinion and American Democracy* (New York: Knopf, 1961), pp. 63–65; and Herbert H. Hyman, "Reflections on Reference Groups," *Public Opinion Quarterly*, XXIV (1960), pp. 383–396.

10 See Dawson, *op. cit.*, pp. 109–116.

11 See *Ibid.*, ch. IV.

12 *Ibid.*, pp. 116–124.

"generation gap" suggested that youth, or maybe age categories were becoming politically relevant reference categories. At present sex may be emerging as a politically relevant reference category.

The importance of various societal groupings as political reference points depends upon two basic criteria. First, it depends upon the strength of identification with particular groupings. The higher the identification and the more cohesive a particular group, the more likely the group is to serve as an important political reference point. Second, the importance of a particular grouping depends upon the relevance of that group for contemporary political issues. The political relevance of a societal grouping depends upon what types of issues are salient at a particular time.

PRIMARY GROUPS AND SECONDARY GROUPS AS SOCIALIZATION AGENTS

DIFFERENCES BETWEEN PRIMARY AND SECONDARY GROUPS

Primary groups are generally small and not highly structured. They entail close, personalized relationships among members. Contact or interaction among members tends to be high and members tend to be concerned with all aspects of each other's lives. The family, close friendship cliques, and close work associates are the best examples of primary groups. Secondary groups tend to include larger numbers of people and to be more highly structured. Relationships within secondary groups are less personal and less intense. Secondary groups generally are concerned with only selected aspects of the lives of individual members.

The distinctions between primary and secondary group relationships might be made clearer by contrasting relationships in groups that will be familiar to the reader. Let us take as examples a small friendship group and a college classroom. The former is a primary group and the latter a secondary group. What are the important differences between these two groups?

Close friends get together often because they like to be with each other. Being together, the relationships they have with each other are valued in themselves. Close friends are generally concerned about all aspects of each other's life — their health and state of mind, how they are doing at school or at work, what they think of current social and political issues, what they want out of life, and so on. Friends often get together with no specific activity or special purpose in mind. It is not unusual for good friends to get together (let us say on a weekend night), and spend a good portion of the evening trying to decide what to do. They are seeking something to do because they want to be together. They are not getting together to accomplish a particular task. "What do you want to do tonight?" "I don't know. What do you want to do?" Such a dialogue can go on for sometime — maybe without ever making a definite decision. The togetherness is the important thing.

Relationships in a school class are quite different. The teacher and the students meet together periodically according to a schedule. There are usually some specific things to be accomplished at each meeting. The students relate to each other and with the teacher primarily with respect to only a few particular roles. For the most part the teacher becomes involved with the students only with regard to their activities and performance as students in that class. Students expect the teacher to judge them on how well they perform in their capacity as students; not on the basis of their inherent goodness, their looks, how they dress, or how much money their parents have. Students, for the most part, relate to the faculty member in his or her capacity as class teacher. This does not mean that other types of relationships do not develop among students or maybe even between teacher and student. The point is that the basic group relationships revolve around the respective teacher-student roles. The rationale for getting together and being involved as a group centers around the same basic relationships. Students and teacher get together for an hour three times a week (or whatever the class meeting schedule might be) not because they particularly value being with each other. The reason for getting together rather rests on the assumption that their being together and engaging in activities such as lectures, discussions, and examinations will permit them to accomplish something else.[13] Learning, earning credits, getting a degree so one can get a good job, earning a living as a faculty member — these are the objectives that bring the class group together at periodic intervals. Unlike the case with primary groups, being together does not generally have great value in itself.

SOURCES OF GROUP INFLUENCE ON INDIVIDUALS

Both primary groups and secondary groups serve as important agents of social and political learning. Political and social attitudes and values are developed, sustained, and/or altered within groups. Why is it that groups have such tremendous influence? Several general reasons can be suggested with respect to how and why groups are so important.[14]

First, groups serve as important communication channels and as such provide the individual with many of the ideas and information he or she obtains. Much of the information an individual receives about the political and social world and many of the attitudes to which he or she is exposed come through group relationships. Close friends pass on ideas and information to each other. One group member obtains some information from outside the group. He or she passes it on to the other group friends. Many secondary groups make an effort to communicate information and group relevant ideas and values to their members and friends. Groups of one type or another are behind most efforts directed toward the adoption or acceptance of particular policies.

Second, groups play a very crucial role in helping define the individual's basic perceptions of the social world. They play a similarly important role in helping to determine the

[13] The point that the creation of some type of social product serves as the basis for the formation of secondary groups while being together is the major value primary group provide their members is made in Scott Greer, *Social Organization* (New York: Random House, 1955), p. 34.

[14] See Darwin Cartwright and Alvin Zander, "Group Pressures and Group Standards: Introduction," in Cartwright and Zander, *op. cit.;* and Leon Festinger, Stanley Schachter, and Kurt Back, *Social Pressures in Informal Groups* (New York: Harper, 1950).

individual's own concept of who he is and how he fits into the social and political world. The self, one's basic perceptions of whom one is, is developed largely through associations with others.[15] The others who are so important in defining the self are usually to be found in the groups with which one is associated. The impact of the family group is particularly important during the early formative years. Play groups during early childhood and peer groups later are also extremely important in this regard. An individual acquires a sense of whether he or she is smart or dumb, competent or not so competent, attractive or not so attractive, by the way others react to him or her. Various secondary groups or organizations — Boy and Girl Scouts, religious youth groups, and a vast array of adult associations — also play roles in defining both the individual and his or her relationship to the social and political world.

Third, groups, both primary and secondary, take positions on issues, articulate those positions to group members and seek to motivate the individual to follow the group position. Individuals take on the positions of the group to which they belong because they like the group members and want to be liked and accepted by the group. In some instances groups have sanctions they will invoke for noncompliance with group norms. Members may be punished in one way or another if they do not follow the norms of the group. Ridicule and threat of expulsion from the group are often extremely potent sanctions that groups can use to enforce compliance with their positions. Punishment or threat of punishment is probably not the most common means through which group norms are accepted. The subtle and not so subtle efforts of individuals to imitate and to follow the position of those with whom they have close associations is probably a more common means through which the group impact is felt.

It should be noted that with respect to each of these sources of influence, primary groups are considerably more likely to influence individuals than are secondary groups. The very

[15] See George Herbert Mead, *Mind, Self, and Society* (Chicago: The University of Chicago Press, 1934).

factors that distinguish primary group relationships make them highly influential with respect to shaping the norms and behavior of their members. The high level of interaction among members means that members have access to each other, an important element in any attempt by a group to communicate or to influence its members. The high level of emotional and personal involvement make it likely that the messages communicated through primary groups will be heeded. Threats of ridicule, disapproval, or ostracism by close friends and associates are extremely effective in enforcing compliance with group standards. The need for approval and to be accepted by those for whom one has strong attachments can be quite strong and as such very potent in motivating and constricting attitudes and behavior. For the most part when primary group influence is pitted against secondary group influence the impact of the primary group is likely to prevail.

THE SPECIAL IMPACT OF PRIMARY GROUPS
IN POLITICAL SOCIALIZATION

Primary groups play a particularly influential role in shaping political orientations. The family, close peer groups, and work associates are important sources of political learning. They serve to transmit and to reinforce particular political outlooks. They provide a context in which political thinking and consciousness are developed and changed. We discussed at some length the impact of the family in political socialization in Chapter VII. The reader should keep in mind that some of the most important primary ties are those formed among family members. Throughout one's life the family provides one with many of one's closest and emotionally involved relationships and as such with some of the most potent socializing influences.[16]

The other important primary group that is important in political and social learning is the peer group. *Peer groups* are a form of primary group composed of members sharing

[16] Herbert McClosky and Harold E. Dahlgren, "Primary Group Influence on Party Loyalty," *American Political Science Review,* LIII (1959), pp. 757–776.

relatively equal status as well as close ties. Peer groups begin to take on special importance during early adolescence. There is some evidence to suggest that during adolescence peer associations begin to replace parents and/or teachers as significant reference figures.[17] Peer relationships continue as important socializing agents throughout the adult period. Their form changes to marriage relationships (husband-wife pairs) and to work and professional colleagues, neighborhood associates, and to primary relationships developed among people in religious and social organizations.

Because peer relationships become important to the individual during and following adolescence they are most important in later political learning. They begin to be important about the time in the life cycle when the substantial developments in basic political outlooks and political knowledge have been achieved. Peer groups are important in the transition period between adolescence and adulthood. They are important in determining when and to what extent the individual will take on various adult political roles, especially more participatory roles. They provide the adult with continuing cues through which he or she understands and adjusts to everyday changes in the political world. They serve either to bolster or to weaken the basic political identities and outlooks that were developed earlier in life. We have suggested in several instances that the earlier identified orientations tend to persist through adulthood. Where they are seriously challenged or altered, where new basic political identities and outlooks are acquired during the adult years the impetus for change often can be traced to changes in close peer associates. The formation of close ties with new people who have different political outlooks is one of the most important mechanisms for bringing about change in political orientations in late adolescence and throughout the adult period. Where significant changes take place during the college years they can often be traced to the impact of new close friends rather

[17] James S. Coleman, *The Adolescent Society* (New York: The Free Press, 1961).

than the college curriculum.[18] Spouses and new job associates may play a similar role in later life.

Friends, individuals with whom one has close personal or primary type relationships, continue to serve as sources of political information and ideas throughout life. When political outlooks remain stable it is usually because they are sustained or reinforced by a network of close primary relationships. When they are weakened or altered it is usually because they are not bolstered or reinforced by existing primary relationships. Despite the largely secondary nature of many social and political relationships, primary groups or primary relationships continue to loom very large in shaping, sustaining, and altering political outlooks.

SECONDARY GROUPS AND POLITICAL SOCIALIZATION

Secondary groups act as agents of political learning in much the same way as peer groups, schools, and the family. They often have political interests and take positions on political issues. They often attempt to educate or pressure their members to follow their political positions. Secondary groups, however, vary greatly in the extent to which they get involved in politics, attempt to influence their members, and the amount of influence they have on individuals.

Secondary groups can have an effect on political socialization in several different ways. (1) They can engage in direct political education and indoctrination efforts. (2) They serve as sources of indirect political learning, especially the apprenticeship type of learning discussed in Chapter VI. (3) They serve as political reference groups somewhat in the way that the societal groupings do, and they often serve to tie individuals in with various societal groupings. (4) They provide a framework in which primary relationships develop, and those primary relationships, in turn, influence political outlooks. The first form of influence is fairly self-evident and does not need further elaboration here. The other three merit brief discussion.

[18] See, for example, R. Middleton and S. Putney, "Student Rebellion Against Parental Political Beliefs," *Social Forces* (1963), pp. 377–383.

One of the important contributions secondary groups make to political learning is to provide experiences and training in group relations and leadership skills that can be transferred to the political world. Participation itself, regardless of the political content and purposes of the group, affects perceptions, skills, and relationships that are relevant for political life. Numerous studies have documented the notion that participation in secondary groups is associated positively with higher levels of political interest, involvement, participation, and with greater sense of political efficacy. Gabriel Almond and Sidney Verba summarize findings from their five-nation study bearing on this notion:

> [Citizens] who are members of a nonpolitical organization are more likely to feel subjectively competent than are those who belong to no organization. This, then, appears to confirm the fact that latent political functions are performed by voluntary associations, whether those organizations are political or not. Those who are members of some organizations, even if they report that it has no political role, have more political competence than those who have no such membership.[19]

Political theorists have long commented on the relevance of voluntary group participation for the operation of liberal democratic societies.[20] The existence of such groups has been accepted by some as a requisite for stable pluralistic democracy. Although secondary groups may, at times, be sources of conflicting influence and action, they help equip individuals with the political attitudes appropriate for democratic politics.[21]

Secondary groups also act as political reference groups. In this sense their influence on ideas and values is similar to that of social groupings. Individuals form identifications with a particular group such as a labor union, a farmers' organiza-

[19] Gabriel Almond and Sidney Verba, *The Civic Culture* (Princeton: Princeton University Press, 1963), p. 309.

[20] See Alexis de Tocqueville, *Democracy In America* II (New York: Vintage Books, 1945), especially pp. 114–118; William Kornhauser, *The Politics of Mass Society* (New York: The Free Press, 1959); and S. M. Lipset et al., *Union Democracy* (New York: The Free Press, 1956).

[21] *Ibid.*

tion, or a religious association, and use that group as a political reference point. They become sensitive to the group's political norms and make political evaluations according to what is best for the group and what it stands for. The same organization can be a positive reference group for some, a negative reference group for others. For the industrial worker, the union is a positive reference group; for the businessman it is a negative reference group. So the industrial worker votes for the union's values and interests, and the businessman is likely to be against anything the union is for. The Communist party has long been a negative reference group for many Americans. In recent years the John Birch Society and the Ku Klux Klan also have become negative reference groups whose support many candidates for public office disavow.

Many primary relationships are formed within the context of secondary groups. Individuals brought together in the activities of a secondary group often form primary ties with one another. Adolescent and youth groups, such as scout troops and student or religious movements, provide youths with contacts that grow into primary groups. Adult primary associations likewise develop within work and social organizations. Secondary groups, thus, structure the individual activity and social relationships that can have such a bearing on political views.

We have outlined various methods through which secondary groups influence the content and structure of the political self. Obviously, the several modes are not mutually exclusive. They often act simultaneously and reinforce each other. The more important the group is for the individual, and the more closely he or she is related to it, the more likely the group is to influence his or her political outlook. The more active the group is in communicating political views, and the more the individual regards the group as politically relevant, the more it shapes political orientations.

Secondary groups are influential particularly during youth and adulthood, as the influence of family and school wanes. For that reason they are most influential for the types of learning that occur after childhood. Secondary groups are important in perpetuating and reinforcing political values related to the social and economic groupings discussed above. In this sense they help maintain the distribution of political orientations linked to the social and demographic structure of societies.

CHAPTER X

Communication Media and Political Experiences

NEWSPAPERS, RADIO, TELEVISION, MAGAZINES, AND OTHER COM-
MUNICATION MEDIA transmit many types of messages that affect
political orientations. Both day-to-day information about political events and evaluations of these events are transmitted
from government to citizen, from group to group, from group
to individual, from elite to nonelite, through the communication media. Political learning may be *active* or *passive,* depending on the extent to which the individual is consciously
involved. Passive learning may take place when there is re-
peated exposure to the same learning stimuli, but the observer
pays little attention.[1] Although one is tempted to suggest that
information and value messages through the communication
media require only passive attention, and are thus less important than active involvement through political experiences,
this may not always be the case. The extent of individual
interest and attentiveness to political messages may be the
important consideration. In this chapter we outline the types
and extent of learning involved in exposures to communication
media and political experiences. We look at the questions:
What is the impact of the media on political socialization?
What are the consequences of political events and political
activities for political socialization?

---

[1] Herbert E. Krugman and Eugene L. Hartley, "Passive Learning from
Television," *Public Opinion Quarterly,* 34 (1970), pp. 184–190.

IMPACT OF COMMUNICATION MEDIA

Communication media play an increasingly important role in our lives. As a result of technological advancements in communication media and the weakening of traditional social structures like the extended family and the local community, the mass media are becoming increasingly important as shapers of political orientations.

The modern nation-state with its common political focus, centralized administration, and widespread participation could not have developed without the advancements in the technology of mass communication.[2] The modern integrated polity cannot exist without widespread, rapid, and generally uniform communication. The rapidity and scope of modern communication was demonstrated vividly at the time of the assassination of President Kennedy in November 1963. Within a few hours almost all Americans knew about the president's death.[3] The news was spread with similar rapidity to nearly all corners of the world. It is accurate to say that most of the world responded simultaneously to a common event.

Even as the mass media are a crucial ingredient for the modern state, they are also an important mechanism through which traditional societies move toward modernity and political integration. Because the mass media can disseminate a consistent and standardized political message simultaneously to vast numbers of people, they can play a key role in the rapid transformation of society. Herbert Hyman points out that in transitional societies, the media, as instruments of socialization, are

> . . . efficient and their sweep is vast enough to cover the huge populations requiring modernization. Their standardization . . . is suited to producing widespread national uniformities in patterns of behavior; and their spirit is modern, no matter what else is wrong with it. By contrast, while the conventional

[2] See Reinhard Bendix, *Max Weber: An Intellectual Portrait* (New York: Doubleday, 1960), Chapters 12–13.

[3] See Paul B. Sheatsley and Jacob J. Feldman, "The Assassination of President Kennedy: A Preliminary Report on Public Reactions and Behavior," *Public Opinion Quarterly*, XXVIII (1964), pp. 192–193.

agencies of socialization in society — parents, teachers, peers, neighbors, and the like — can be more flexible in suiting the lesson to the capacities and needs of the particular learner and more potent an influence, the outcomes cannot be as uniform, and their efforts are often directed against modernization.[4]

Hyman is correct in stressing the potential utility of mass media for the tasks of modernization and integration, but their potential in this capacity is easily overrated. The same societies that Hyman believes require standardized socialization are those that lack the technical skills and facilities to use the mass media effectively. The nations most in need of such modernizing communication are those least likely to have such resources. Their populations often are illiterate, possess few radios and television sets, and are inattentive to the political content of media communications.

The mass media are more prevalent and effective as instruments of communication and socialization in more modern societies.[5] This point is testified to by data presented in Table X.1. The mass media, particularly television and movies, are the most frequently mentioned sources of information about foreign people for children in the modern nations, for example, the United States, Canada, Germany, and Japan. In the less well developed societies — Bantu (Republic of South Africa), Brazil, Israel, Lebanon, and Turkey — television is not mentioned at all. Parents and friends are the most frequently mentioned information sources. France is the only important exception to this pattern. France is a highly developed nation in an economic sense, but it follows the patterns of the less developed nations in regard to information sources. Even as these data suggest differences in communication patterns between modern and nonmodern societies, they attest to an important role for the mass media, especially television, in more highly developed nations. The communication media

4 Herbert H. Hyman, "Mass Communication and Political Socialization: The Role of Patterns of Communications," in Lucien Pye (ed.), *Communications and Political Development* (Princeton: Princeton University Press, 1963), p. 143.

5 See Richard R. Fagen, *Politics and Communication* (Boston: Little, Brown, 1966), pp. 53–69.

TABLE X.I *Comparisons of Popularly Used Sources of Information (about Foreign People)*

	American	Bantu	Brazilian	English-Canadian	French	French-Canadian	German	Israeli	Japanese	Lebanese	Turkish
						Nationality of Children					
6-year-olds	TV[a] movies (parents)	parents	parents (contact)	TV,[b] contact	parents	TV[b]	parents, TV-movies (contact)	parents, friends	parents, TV-movies	contact, parents	parents, friends
10- and 14-year-olds	TV-movies, books, courses, texts, magazines	parents, (10 yrs. only), contact,[c] teachers	movies, magazines, contact	TV, courses, texts, books	parents, (10 yrs. only), texts, books, magazines (14 yrs. only)	TV, texts, books, magazines (14 yrs. only)	TV-movies, books, magazines courses, contact, radio	books, friends, courses, movies, magazines	TV-movies, courses, texts, teachers, magazines	books, magazines, radio, movies, texts, friends, contact	books, texts, courses, movies, magazines

Source: *Children's Views of Foreign Peoples, A Cross-National Study,* by Wallace E. Lambert and Otto Klineberg. Copyright © 1967. Reprinted by permission of Irvington Publishers, Inc.

a Listed in approximate order of frequency. Those in parentheses are not as frequently mentioned as the others.

b Since children in Montreal are not allowed to attend movie theatres until they are sixteen years of age, it was presumed that television was the major source coded in the TV-movies category.

c Refers to direct contact or exposure to foreign people.

serves a linkage function in binding the nation-state together. By disseminating political information and values it can be a potent force in political socialization. The question is to what extent the media does perform this role in political learning?

THE MEDIA AS A SHAPER OF POLITICAL ORIENTATIONS

Generally the mass media has been assigned a secondary role in political socialization. There does not seem to be data to warrant the conception of the mass media as a primary shaper of political attitudes. Yet, the media *do* have obvious effects on people's thinking and general behavior. We suggest that the media does have a role in both childhood and adult learning.

There has been extensive research on the media's effect on the child's values and behavior. Much of the research has centered on the relationship between media violence and its behavioral effects.[6] Learning by observation and imitation, as discussed in Chapter VI, is a critical aspect of the child's social learning process. It would seem that any steady diet of television would have the potential of exerting a powerful influence on children. According to the 1970 census, 96 percent of all American homes contain at least one television set. Most children watch TV from fourteen to forty-nine hours a week, depending on age and social and economic background. They develop established patterns of favorite programs and viewing times, often by age three.[7] Given the time a child spends in front of the television set (often more time than in front of a teacher in a year's period), the potentialities of the media as a socializing and teaching agent are great. "Research has shown that the simple observation of others can be very potent in changing such widely varied aspects of social behavior as a child's willingness to aid others, and his learning of lan-

6 See Alberta Siegel, "The Effects of Media Violence on Social Learning," in Victor B. Cline (ed.), *Where Do You Draw The Line?: An Exploration into Media Violence, Pornography, and Censorship* (Utah: Brigham Young University Press, 1974), pp. 129–146.

7 See Victor B. Cline, Rogert G. Croft, and Steven Courrier, "The Desensitization of Children to T.V. Violence," in Cline, *op. cit.*, pp. 147–155.

guage." [8] Television's *Sesame Street* revolutioned preschool learning of the alphabet. Television does much less in the area of political learning.

As discussed in Chapter VI, children learn values and attitudes, which may be transferred later to political objects. In much the same way that a child observes violence on entertainment television and becomes more aggressive in his or her attitudes and behavior,[9] a child can take more positive messages from the media and learn valuable lessons of good citizenship. More often, however, television is not geared to play an active role in political learning. Given commercial interests, the media do not take advantage of this opportunity to directly teach positive political values and attitudes.

The media can be consequential in shaping adult's views also. The media can shape political orientations by supplying new information and creating new images of political leaders. Once again, the potentialities for shaping political attitudes exists, but is not much used. Political candidates have come to rely more and more on the exposure of television. The Nixon-Kennedy debates in 1960 allowed Kennedy to emerge as a viable political competitor to the then better-known vice-president of the United States. Kennedy was able to create an image of leadership for the American public. Nixon's better use of the mass media in controlled, regulated television performances in 1968, allowed him to emerge from political defeat as an elder statesman and leader. Senator Muskie's publicized emotional outburst in defense of his wife in 1968 is said to have cost him the nomination. The 1976 presidential election also centered around the use of television. Political leaders realize the potency of television as an image creator.[10]

The media also may develop a political consensus where none existed. In modern times, the extensive coverage of

[8] Robert M. Liebert, Emily S. Davidson, and John M. Neale, "Aggression in Childhood: The Impact of Television," in Cline, *Ibid.*, pp. 114.

[9] *Ibid.*, p. 120.

[10] See Dan Nimmo and Robert L. Savage, *Candidates and Their Images: Concepts, Methods, and Findings* (California: Goodyear Publishing Company, 1976).

"Watergate" helped to shape political attitudes. Although newspaper coverage of the bits and pieces of Watergate emerged over time, the extensive television coverage of the Senate hearings on Watergate and the House impeachment hearings had a dramatic impact on public opinion. The oft restated questions concerning President Nixon's guilt: "What he knew and when he knew it," became translated into a consensus that Nixon could no longer lead the country. One of the effects of Watergate (transmitted through the media), was the decline in support for the President.[11]

FACTORS AFFECTING MEDIA IMPACT

In evaluating mass media as a political socialization agency, four observations are relevant. First, more often than not the media act as transmitters of political cues originated by other agencies. Second, the information carried by mass media goes through a two-step flow. Third, the media tend to reinforce existing political orientations rather than create new ones. Fourth, the messages of the mass media are received and interpreted in a social setting, and in the context of socially conditioned predispositions.

Many of the politically relevant messages transmitted through radio, television, newspapers, and other communication media have their origins outside the media. Government officials and political leaders make statements; secondary groups transmit political information to their members; events in the political world are picked up and communicated to large populations. The media serve mainly as the instrument through which these socialization agencies communicate their messages. The directors of mass media may, in fact, have only a limited say in what sort of political data they transmit to the population.

A number of communication studies have found that mass communication media do not tend to influence the masses of

[11] See a discussion of this point in Fred I. Greenstein, "The Benevolent Leader Revisited: Children's Images of Political Leaders in Three Democracies," *The American Political Science Review*, 69 (December 1975), pp. 1393–1397.

the population directly.[12] Messages coming through the media first reach a small number of "opinion leaders" who are particularly attentive to the media. By word of mouth, opinion leaders such as teachers, ministers, and community activists, then pass on the messages to those over whom they are influential. Mass media messages, thus, tend to flow in two steps. The opinion leader is the crucial person; he or she usually influences a small group of close friends. Elihu Katz describes the relationship as follows:

> Opinion leaders and the people whom they influence are very much alike and typically belong to the same primary groups of family, friends and co-workers. While the opinion leader may be more interested in the particular sphere in which he is influential, it is highly unlikely that the person influenced will be very far behind the leader in their level of interest.[13]

The two-step flow of communication places additional emphasis upon the family and peer groups as influential agents of political learning. Only a minority of persons follow the media closely, especially the political communications there. Those who do are important in communicating the messages to those who do not. In the process, of course, the message gets reinterpreted and transformed by the opinion leaders.

On the whole, the mass media serve to reinforce and to crystallize existing orientations rather than to alter old ones or to create new ones. As one student of communications' influence points out: "A number of studies, some performed in the laboratory and some in the social world, indicate that persuasive mass communication functions far more frequently as an agent of reinforcement than as an agent of change." [14] In his study of public opinion, V. O. Key sets this observation in a larger social context. He points out that: ". . . it is safe

[12] For summaries of this work, see Elihu Katz, "The Two-Step Flow of Communication: An Up-to-Date Report on an Hypothesis," *Public Opinion Quarterly*, XXI (1957), pp. 61–78; and Elihu Katz and Paul F. Lazarsfeld, *Personal Influence* (New York: The Free Press, 1955).

[13] Katz, *Ibid.*, p. 77.

[14] Joseph T. Klopper, *The Effects of Mass Communication* (New York: The Free Press, 1960), p. 15.

to conclude that the major influence of the media upon political attitudes is by and large a reinforcement of the status quo." [15]

This reinforcement of existing orientations results in part from the nature of communication messages. Major messages are designed for the most part to support existing arrangements and to convey interpretations considered appropriate by social power holders. This reinforcement function results also from tendencies on the part of the receiver. People are more apt to be attentive to the media when they agree with what they are being told. During a political campaign people pay attention to the speeches of the candidates they already support. A study of the effect of an educational campaign on the United Nations, for example, found that those who noticed the campaign were those who were most favorably disposed toward the United Nations before the campaign.[16] Those not favorable to the United Nations, the ones whom the campaign set out to influence, tended not to notice or be affected by the educational effort. The communication media, consequently, are *not* the most effective means of converting persons to new ideas. Messages may be sent out, but there is no way of insuring they will reach those to whom they are directed. Katz and Paul Lazarsfeld offer the following conclusion about the persuasive influence of the media:

> Perhaps the most important generalization in this area — at least as far as understanding the process of effective persuasion is concerned — is that those groups which are most hopefully regarded as the target of a communication are often least likely to be in the audience.[17]

As the two-step flow of communication hypothesis suggests, messages from the mass media are seldom received and interpreted by isolated individuals. The reaction to mass media communications are influenced by the social location of the individual receiving them. Both the individual's preconcep-

15 V. O. Key, Jr., *Public Opinion and American Democracy* (New York: Knopf, 1961), p. 396.

16 A. Star and H. M. Hughes, "Report on an Educational Campaign: The Cincinnati Plan for the United Nations," *American Journal of Sociology*, LV (1950), pp. 389–440.

17 Katz and Lazarsfeld, *op. cit.*, pp. 21–22.

tions and his immediate social setting influence the impact that mass media will have on him.[18] First, the social setting helps determine which media and communications the individual will be exposed to. Second, the social setting affects the way in which the individual interprets and reacts to particular messages. "It is obvious that mass communication is a social process — a social person interacts with others, participates in cooperative social activities."[19] This observation again stresses the importance of primary associations and personal influence in the development of political outlooks.

These four qualifications constitute a brief outline of factors relevant to the socialization influence of mass communication media. By and large they suggest that the media affect the development of attitudes and opinions primarily in conjunction with other agents of socialization, especially small, personal groups. The communication media are important in carrying numerous political messages, the most important of which are news about everyday political events. In addition, the media convey, both directly and indirectly, the major consensus values of the society. Media acts to crystallize and reinforce lessons passed on by the family, schools, peers, and other agents of political learning.

POLITICAL EVENTS AND POLITICAL EXPERIENCES

Although exposure to political messages through the media tends to involve a more passive attitude on the part of the audience, political events and experiences often involve a more active participation. This form of learning also involves both a shaping and a reinforcement of earlier predispositions. Political events may affect both children and adults, although to different degrees. Political experience is more important for adult socialization when the opportunities for participating are more extensive. Political experiences and political events are obviously most important for those who have an interest in politics. Political events are less likely to influence

---

[18] See Eliot Friedson, "The Relation of the Social Situation of Contact to the Media in Mass Communication," *Public Opinion Quarterly,* XVII (1953), pp. 230–238.

[19] *Ibid.,* p. 230.

people who are isolated from the political mainstream and those who have only minimal perceptions of the political world. Citizens with higher levels of political consciousness, when politics is more salient and important, would also tend to follow political events and be more likely to get involved in political experiences.

POLITICAL EVENTS AS A SHAPER OF PUBLIC OPINION

Political events may have a direct impact on political perceptions and values. Political learning, quite obviously, does not occur in isolation from the world of politics. The shootings at Kent State University in the heat of the "antiwar" effort had repercussions across college campuses. As described in Chapter IV, Watergate affected children's attitudes toward the president, but had increasing effect according to age. Older children expressed more negative feelings toward the president than younger children.[20] As children mature and develop the ability to understand more abstract political relationships, political events tend to affect them more.

In the adult population the drastic decrease in feelings of political responsiveness and political trust since 1964, described in Chapter V, is another indication of the effect of political events. In the last decade the American people have developed a mounting distrust of their national government. The Vietnam War and the government "credibility gap" associated with it, court-ordered integration efforts and its ensuing forced bussing, inflation and high unemployment, and the exposés associated with Watergate and the Nixon administration have all combined to bring about a lack of confidence in the national government. The unfolding of Watergate events may have only *reinforced* what some people felt about the administration of President Nixon, but the psychological impact on the country as a whole was great.

POLITICAL EXPERIENCES

During one's early years the maturing citizen learns *about* a political world with which he or she has little direct contact

[20] See Table V.1.

and few direct relationships. Many of the lessons about politics are learned by the child in anticipation of his rights and responsibilities as an adult. On the whole, political experiences come after basic political learning is accomplished. The child is taught by family and schools what voting is, but only as an adult does he or she actually vote. We do not mean to imply that the child has no direct experience with the political world. He or she is familiar with some political symbols and personalities and hears about some political events. Nevertheless, such experiences are not the major aspect of early political learning.

By late adolescence and after, political experiences themselves enter the stage to help shape the political self. The individual begins to learn directly from the political world instead of only about it. Political leaders attempt to influence his or her attitudes by speeches, announcements, and propaganda campaigns. Voting, attending political meetings, dealing with governmental officials, provide important lessons for the individual citizen.

To some extent adult experiences in the political world are a sort of testing of reality. In childhood and youth the citizen is taught many things about his political world. This learning later is tested by his or her actual experiences. As a child he may be taught that political leaders are wise and benevolent; that he should trust, respect, and obey them. In later experiences he finds they make unwise decisions and do not treat citizens fairly. The child is taught in school that the policeman is a friendly, fair, and trustworthy helper. Later experiences at the hands of the law may teach him that the police are brutal and dishonest. Of course, political experiences are not always disenchanting. A young man may be taught by his father that governmental bureaucrats will not listen to him, and that it is useless to expect any services from them. The youth, with more education and social status than his father, may learn later how to approach public officials and find them responsive to his petitions. But given the nature of official political education in most nations, with its tendency to simplify and glorify the political images presented, actual political experiences are more likely to develop cynicism than vice versa.

Studies of American school children find that children tend to have positive, benevolent attitudes toward political authority figures.[21] They are not cynical about government. Political cynicism, however, is widespread among American adults.[22] Another seeming anomaly is that lower class children more frequently accept authority figures as right and depend on their trustworthiness.[23] But among the adult population it is the citizens of higher status who demonstrate more trust and have the more positive attitudes toward governmental effectiveness and toward their own efficacy in the political world. There appears, then, to be a reversal in class tendencies between childhood and adulthood, with lower status citizens becoming more cynical and less positive about the political world. We suggest that this reversal results in part from the different experiences upper and lower status persons have in the political and social world. The experiences of lower status citizens lead them to become more cynical about politics and less sure about their ability to influence the political world. The political experiences of higher status persons, on the other hand, lead them to become more positive and to develop a greater sense of political efficacy because they have been more successful.

Political experiences are obviously most important for those who have an interest in politics. There are data suggesting that the political activists tend to have political values somewhat different from the rest of the population.[24] Key proposes the existence of a political activist subculture made up of the

21 See Fred I. Greenstein, *Children and Politics* (New Haven: Yale University Press, 1965), pp. 31–42.

22 Robert E. Aggar, Marshall Goldstein, and Stanley Pearl, "Political Cynicism: Meaning and Measurements," *Journal of Politics,* XXIII (1961), pp. 477–506.

23 Robert D. Hess and Judith Torney, *The Development of Political Attitudes in Children* (Chicago: Aldine, 1967).

24 See especially Robert McClosky, "Consensus and Ideology in American Politics," *American Political Science Review,* LVIII (1964), pp. 361–382.

minority of citizens who are particularly attentive to and active in politics.[25] He suggests that this minority has more confidence in democratic procedures than the rest of society. If this is true, it probably follows that experiences in the political world, as well as experiences with socialization agents, play an especially important part in forming views of the political activists.

We discussed in Chapter VI ways in which political experiences shape the political self. To summarize: political events and experiences in the political world are particularly important for the political learning that takes place during the adult years. Political socialization of this type is most significant for the readjustments the individual makes with the changing political world. His or her experiences serve to correct or complete the political learning that took place during the preadult years. Learning from political experiences and events is most important for the politically attentive and active.

[25] Key, *op. cit.,* pp. 536–538.

CHAPTER XI

Concluding Thoughts

WHY DO STUDENTS OF POLITICS study *when* and *how* children and adults acquire their political outlooks? It is because they believe the study of political socialization can tell them some things about the way in which politics works — things that might otherwise remain unexplained. The claim is not that political socialization studies tell us all or even most of what we want to know about political life, only that they tell us enough to make the inquiry worthwhile.

These concluding thoughts are intended to draw together some of the themes developed in this text and to illustrate how the inquiry into political socialization helps us understand the complex, often bewildering political life around us. Two topics are singled out for attention: (1) political change and (2) political obedience. By briefly considering these topics we can review some of the arguments and findings already presented, as well as suggest the utility of studying political socialization.

POLITICAL CHANGE

The changes that take place in societies are among the oldest and least understood of social phenomena. Students of society have long sought adequate explanations of social and political change, but no satisfactory, comprehensive theory has been developed. In the latter part of the twentieth century, we are still searching for explanations of the mechanisms that transform one network of social relations, one pattern of cultural values, into another. What processes cause, or permit, new generations of citizens to break sharply with the political outlooks of their predecessors? What mechanisms make such breaks difficult and unlikely? Political socialization theory points us toward some of the mechanisms of social evolution, as well as toward conditions that make social change difficult and uneven.

One of the major propositions about change is that centrally directed cultural change is enormously difficult to bring about. Many governments have attempted to transform what their citizens believe: the Soviet Union in the 1920s, China in the 1950s, Tanzania in the 1960s. These exercises in social and political transformation have met with limited success. Often, they have been accompanied by political violence aimed at purging "revisionist" thinking — those who clung to the older outlooks, or in other ways deviated from the new official line.

Political socialization theory helps us to understand why centrally directed cultural change is so difficult. In the previous section we discussed the various agents that contribute to political socialization. One of the major points of that section is that political ideas are transmitted and political thinking is nutured through a wide variety of associations. The agents of political socialization include small personalized groups such as the family and peer groups that are not easily controlled and manipulated by political officials, as well as school curricula and political propaganda that often contain officially sanctioned political messages. Much of political learning is not carefully programmed from above. Some takes place without any conscious intent from the agent doing the socializing.

Much of what an individual learns about politics is learned from socialization agencies and social experiences that are only indirectly linked to the formal political system. The family and peer groups in particular are important in shaping political outlooks. They lie beyond the direct control and manipulation of political authorities. This situation makes for certain resistance to programmed change. Political engineers, political educators, and political propagandists quickly learn about the potency and the rigidity of the informal network in political socialization. Political elites can manipulate only at the edges of these processes. Textbooks can be changed or re-written, political propaganda in the mass media can be altered; but much important political learning occurs through agencies that can be reprogrammed neither quickly nor effectively.

The spector of *1984* notwithstanding, neither twentieth-century totalitarian regimes, political leaders in new nations, nor democratic devotees promoting increased political par-ticipation have found it easy to alter radically political views and habits. What parents pass on to child, teacher to student, or friend to friend concerning the political world remains unprogrammed. The experiences people have with politics in some instances may be even less manipulatable. To convince a population that the political order is efficient, some efficiency must be demonstrated. Political propaganda cannot replace the tangible experiences citizens have.

In general there is a conservative bias in political socializa-tion. To the extent that changes in political values are depend-ent on political socialization processes, we expect alterations to be incremental rather than galloping. Changes will tend to be uneven rather than consistent and systematic. Before leaving this observation, we should append one major quali-fication. It is not in error to say that political socialization is a conserving force, but neither is it completely accurate. It is more accurate to suggest that political socialization is a mold-ing force. Man is fairly plastic. The very notion of the "social self," from which is drawn the idea of the political self, im-plies this. It is true that in the overwhelming number of cases social institutions are geared to producing citizens who more or less replicate their predecessors. In this sense political social-ization is conservative. But there is nothing inherent in the process to make it so. The powerful molding possibilities in political socialization can be adapted to radical and total alter-ations as well — although maybe not as easily as they have been adapted to incremental changes and protection of the social order.

Cases of individual transformation are well known. Psychi-

atric case histories and religious literature testify to the possibility of total conversion. Although it is more difficult to find
examples of cultures than individuals undergoing total
change, such examples are available. It is important that their
rarity not obscure their theoretical importance. We can briefly
cite two relevant cases.

The history of the American Negro is a case of radical cultural transformation. In a matter of a generation or two, the
Negro, brought to work the cotton plantations, ceased to
resemble his more fortunate African brethren who avoided the
slave market. The experience of being enslaved all but anni-
hilated the slave's cultural past. The enslavement process was
a series of severe shocks: capture in native wars or raiding
parties, the long march to the seaport, sale to slave traders, the
dread middle passage, the humiliation of the market in the
West Indies, and the chattel status, which meant total denial
of any human rights.

Only one out of three West Africans survived this horren-
dous journey. The survivors quickly discovered that the old
values no longer had any meaning. A completely new life,
separated from the previous life by a series of terrible experiences, meant that the old ways had to be discarded. We sus-
pect that the first generation slave did not really "forget" his
name, his family, his religion, his homeland, his language. But
he found them irrelevant to his new status. Survival depended
on the slave master, and he was not often tolerant of the
"primitive" cultural forms of the slave's native West Africa. It
is small wonder that native culture was discarded and that
the American Negro bears so little resemblance to his African
forebears.

Another, more recent example of extreme cultural transformation occurred in the Nazi concentration camps. Studies of
the effects of German concentration camp experiences present
a bleak picture. Inmates who survived the arrest in the middle
of the night, cattle-car transportation, initial platform "selec-
tion," indignities of the SS guards, frequent physical pain,
constant psychological tensions, loss of the past, and bewilder-
ment about the future, underwent profound personality
changes. The concentration camp inmate bore little resem-

blance to the free man he once had been. Nor is the man who returned to "normal" life after the concentration camp simply an extension of his childhood years. The intervening experience was too awful to forget.

The lessons of American slavery and German concentration camps are an important corrective to any tendency to impute conservatism as a necessary component of political socialization. Under conditions of severe dislocation, man can undergo extensive personality and cultural alteration. Circumstances can bring about massive changes in political views. The fact that the informality and diffuseness of the political socialization process make it difficult to transform cultural patterns does not mean such transformation is impossible.

POLITICAL OBEDIENCE

Politics involves the organization and operation of power and authority in society. Politics thereby involves issues of citizen obedience and compliance. Why do people obey laws? Especially, why do they obey laws that harm their own well-being, such as giving up hard-earned money by paying taxes, submitting to the unpleasant rigors of military training, and following regulations that cut into the profits of business?

Three answers are usually given to queries about why people obey: (1) They fear that disobedience will result in punishment — as indeed it often does, which is why societies have police forces, courts of law, prisons, and the rest of the apparatus of punishment. (2) They are bribed into obedience — that is, by obeying laws, citizens feel their own interests will be furthered in the long run (this is the specific support we made reference to in Chapter II, in the discussion of systems theory). (3) Citizens feel it is right and appropriate to obey laws, even those they disagree with or that seem unlikely to ever benefit them — either directly or indirectly.

This third reason for obedience introduces the notion of authority. Power is "authorized" or "legitimate" when the exercise of it is considered right, acceptable, and appropriate. We usually say that the government has *authority* to command us, not that it has the *power* to command us (although it clearly has the latter as well). Legitimated authority was discussed in Chapter II, where we looked at two broad theories of political socialization: the systems theory of diffuse support and the hegemonic theory of induced acquiescence.

Citizen obedience based on acceptance of power as authoritative is an aspect of politics that can be illuminated in political socialization studies. We have drawn on ideas from Jean Piaget (see Chapter III) to consider how political socialization involves, first, learning to obey authority, and, subsequently, discovering how to play a part in its direction and manipulation.

Early childhood development can be characterized as movement from a stage in which there is no recognition of rules and authority to a second stage in which rules are recognized as absolute — directed by some higher authority. This development is relevant for political socialization. Without obedience or adherence to authority, there is no social order. Unless a child learns to obey rules and regulations, he cannot take his place as a citizen in the adult world. Thus it is that adults teach children that obedience to authority is necessary and generally good. A child's first contact with government is characterized by this recognition of authority, of rules, of the necessity of obedience. Political objects are positive and emotionally charged. It is "good" to be good. Being good is being obedient. The law-abiding basis of adult citizenship is laid early. Only later in the development of the political self do other views of authority take their place along with compliance.

As the child leaves the exclusive family circle and moves into peer groups and into the classroom, his or her experiences with authority undergo a subtle but significant change. Rules come to be seen as conventions, as something agreed upon although sometimes arbitrary. The child finds it is possible to ask questions about the rules. Rules cease to have the absolute character they once had. Authorities "justify" their orders. We do not wish to exaggerate this point, however. Teachers continue to say, "Do this because I say so." Power and authority remain mixed in the mind of the child. Nevertheless, the political socialization process is expanded to include other types of learning experiences, other perceptions of authority. We can see this trend accelerated, in particular, as we move from childhood into adolescence. Learning shifts from situations in which the learner is always submissive to situations in which he or she may be an equal. A new view of authority may come about first in peer groups, in which relationships are more spontaneous and rules less rigid and prevalent.

From a recognition of the conventional nature of rules comes another stage: the recognition that rules are changeable, that they can be influenced and manipulated. This recognition begins in adolescence and is accelerated during early adulthood. We have cited the significance of extracurricular activities and participation in classroom decision making in earlier chapters. In addition, the political content of high school curricula tends to stress the participatory rights of individuals, in contrast to the passive duties of individuals stressed in lower grades. Authorities become somewhat redefined. Rather than distant, unapproachable law givers, they become responsible and responsive leaders. Discussions of accountability replace instructions in obedience. As adolescence gives way to adulthood, this notion that authority is somewhat under the control or influence of the average citizen is even more prevalent. It is during the adult years that a person actually learns how to participate in politics, how to make his or her influence felt, how to voice demands, how to combine his or her claims with similar claims of others to maximize influence. Very often this learning takes place through doing.

The development of the citizen, from this perspective, can be viewed as a series of changes in attitudes toward power and authority. At the earliest stage, political learning stresses the "given" nature of authority. Later the stress is on the "conventional" nature, and still later the emphasis shifts to the "accountable" and "participatory" nature of authority. A basic and enduring respect for the political order is the foundation upon which orientations about the manipulability of specific rules are built.

The reader may think of many examples that contradict the picture presented here. It is clearly an idealized version of socialization into a participatory society. Not all societies

worry about whether their citizens believe they can play a
role in governance. Even in those societies formally committed
to democratic values, not all citizens benefit from the type of
socialization just described. Indeed, as we saw in the discussion of American schools, some commentators feel that the
authoritarian structure of American education prevents adolescents from ever developing a meaningful understanding of
citizenship in a democracy.

Qualifications notwithstanding, the developmental profile
of attitudes toward obedience helps us understand our question: why do people obey political authority? The question is
particularly critical in a democracy. The democratic philosophy informs the citizen that he is not obliged to conform to
the law unless the law is generally to his liking. From Locke,
from Rousseau, from Jefferson, indeed from the entire democratic tradition, we learn that democracies are built on the
notion of "contingent obligation." A philosophy of *contingent
obligation* means that the citizen can decide. "This is not for
me, I'll emigrate (or secede)." Or, "I think I'll not pay taxes
this year"; or "I'm tired of obeying traffic signals"; or "I refuse
to be drafted." Needless to say, a system built upon the idea of
contingent obligation might be a fragile one indeed.

We might ask then if democratic states practice what they
preach. Does the citizen really believe in contingent obligation? Political socialization theory provides a partial answer
and in so doing provides a clue to why some democracies operate as effectively as they often do.

We have seen that the young citizen first learns the lesson
of obedience as submission and only later learns that authority
is conventional; not until adulthood does he really discover
that he can participate in the making of binding decisions. It
is critical here that the *first* lesson is that of unquestioned
obedience. If we recall other material presented in the previous chapters, it is clear that another major lesson is learned at
the same time as the lesson of obedience. This is the lesson of
loyalty. Indeed, and this is the crux of the issue, the lessons of
obedience and loyalty are indistinguishable. Children are
taught to obey authority and to love their country at the same
time and by the same models of behavior. They come to be-

lieve that it is "good" to "obey." The psychological link between obedience and loyalty in the mind of the citizen is
significant for the way in which the political society operates.

First, of all the mechanisms that might induce obligation,
political socialization is the cheapest and most efficient. We
noted that people obey because they fear the consequence of
disobedience, or because they consider it worth their while to
obey, or because they consider compliance the appropriate behavior. The third reason is the product of the type of political
socialization processes discussed here. Fear and expedience, the
alternative methods of inducing compliance, are expensive in
comparison. Police states must spend a great deal on institutions that keep the populace in line. Expedience can be nearly
as expensive. Under such conditions, authorities must con-
tinually make it worthwhile for the citizen to obey, and the
"worth" in "worthwhile" comes dear. But compliance based
on the feeling that obedience is "good" or "appropriate" is
cheap. When authorities can depend on such a mechanism,
they can direct resources and energies toward other goals.

Another implication is equally critical. This consequence of
a political socialization process linking obedience to loyalty
can also be viewed from the perspective of the citizen rather
than the authorities. Democratic philosophy insists on the
rights of minorities. Theoretically, one of the minority rights,
by no means an unimportant one, is secession. A sizable minority in any democratic national system that becomes dis-
satisfied with the political order should be able to opt out.

Of course, secession as a tenet of democratic ideology conflicts with the demands of nationalism. Nationalism insists on
protecting the integrity of the territorial boundaries. Neither
encroachments from without nor mass emigration from within
nor secession of any geographical entity is tolerable to the
nation-state. In a very real sense, "compulsory citizenship" is
not unknown in democratic nations.

How do citizens, especially members of potentially dis-
gruntled minority groups, come to accept compulsory citizenship? Few American blacks, for example, speak of leaving the
national system. Findings presented earlier provide the answer
to this question. Compulsory citizenship is made tolerable

because the sense of loyalty to the nation-state is deeply imbedded. The basic inconsistency between democratic philosophy and nationalistic ideology is infrequently perceived by the citizen, and even less frequently acted upon. The multitude of political socialization agencies are largely responsible for creating and sustaining the sense of patriotism that conveniently connects obedience and loyalty.

As our summarizing framework indicates, the citizen does eventually learn that authority is not "given," but is accountable. But by the time he discovers this, his ties with the nation are firmly cemented. In the overwhelming majority of cases citizens do not revolt against the political order, even when the official ideology gives them this right.

In other words, the remarkable thing about democracies is that in assuming a policy of contingent obligation, they generate so few problems of disaffection and withdrawal. The reason for this is that most nations really do not permit the citizen's sense of obligation to be contingent. Political socialization mechanisms replace fear or purchase as a way of maintaining citizenship loyalty. The earliest models of citizenship — parents, teachers, youth leaders, ministers — are models of obedience. Our cultural heroes are not those who violate the norms but those who uphold them. Citizens become bound to the political community with such psychological tenacity that the option of noncompliance is seldom raised.

Our concluding remarks on political change and political obedience serve to remind us that the study of political socialization aids theorizing about politics at two levels: (1) at the individual level we achieve a clearer sense of how people come to think and behave as they do politically; (2) at the national level we begin to see how millions of individual political thoughts and acts add up to broad patterns of political stability or instability, political compliance or defiance, political continuity or change. Although much work needs to be done on how to "add up" individual political socialization experiences, this is where the greatest pay-off will come to the student of politics.

Index